POCKET DICTIONARY *of the*
REFORMED TRADITION

KELLY M. KAPIC &
WESLEY VANDER LUGT

IVP Academic

An imprint of InterVarsity Press
Downers Grove, Illinois

InterVarsity Press
P.O. Box 1400, Downers Grove, IL 60515-1426
World Wide Web: www.ivpress.com
Email: email@ivpress.com

InterVarsity Press® is the book-publishing division of InterVarsity Christian Fellowship/USA®, a movement of students and faculty active on campus at hundreds of universities, colleges and schools of nursing in the United States of America, and a member movement of the International Fellowship of Evangelical Students. For information about local and regional activities, write Public Relations Dept., InterVarsity Christian Fellowship/USA, 6400 Schroeder Rd., P.O. Box 7895, Madison, WI 53707-7895, or visit the IVCF website at www.intervarsity.org.

Cover design: Cindy Kiple
Interior design: Beth Hagenberg
Image: Reformed tradition: Roberta Polfus

ISBN 978-0-8308-2708-4 (print)
ISBN 978-0-8308-8443-8 (digital)

Printed in the United States of America ∞

InterVarsity Press is committed to protecting the environment and to the responsible use of natural resources. As a member of Green Press Initiative we use recycled paper whenever possible. To learn more about the Green Press Initiative, visit www.greenpressinitiative.org.

Library of Congress Cataloging-in-Publication Data

Kapic, Kelly M., 1972-
Pocket dictionary of the Reformed tradition / Kelly M. Kapic, Wesley Vander Lugt.
pages cm. — (IVP pocket reference series)
Includes bibliographical references.
ISBN 978-0-8308-2708-4 (pbk. : alk. paper)
1. Reformed Church—Dictionaries. I. Vander Lugt, Wesley, 1981- II. Title.
BX9406.K37 2013
284'.203—dc23

2013003933

P 20 19 18 17 16 15 14 13 12 11 10 9 8 7 6 5 4 3 2 1
Y 30 29 28 27 26 25 24 23 22 21 20 19 18 17 16 15 14 13

To Todd Capen and Jeff Weigum
Thank you for teaching me the faith in love,
passion and humility
Kelly

To my parents,
Gaylen and Marla Vander Lugt
For passionately upholding and consistently
demonstrating the richness of
the Reformed tradition
Wes

Preface

WE ALL LIKE TO KNOW AND BE KNOWN. Consequently, when situations arise in which we do not understand what we are reading or hearing, we easily become overwhelmed. This is true for all of us, whether we are in the classroom or at a dinner.

For example, when students are just beginning their studies in biology, all the terms and background information easily discourage the newcomer. Such feelings of disorientation are often forgotten after we have learned a skill or subject, but the novice experiences this intensely. In such situations, wise biology teachers remember what it was like when everything was new and they had little background knowledge. With that in mind, they slowly begin to teach through the basics—explaining key scientific theories and specialized vocabulary. During this process the goal is neither to learn the complexity of all the principles immediately nor to grasp the exhaustive history of the language at the outset, but rather to enter into the conversation through basic summaries and guidelines. After a season, the student is equipped and able to dive more deeply, learning some of the qualifications, complications and debates that go along with the theories and history of the subject at hand.

Theological traditions often work in the same way. When one is raised or trained in a particular tradition, the common sights and sounds are easily taken for granted. But for the newcomer, all this is overwhelming and can create obstacles to profitable understanding.

Few theological traditions are as complex, rich and varied as the Reformed tradition. This is a rewarding heritage that has sustained and fostered the faith of many Christians through the centuries and around the globe. Yet it is easily misunderstood and misrepresented, by both insiders and outsiders. For example, sometimes John Calvin is viewed as the devil, and sometimes he is treated in messianic ways. Both views are problematic and false. We must know at least a little about Calvin if we are to understand and appreciate this tradition, but Calvin is only one person, and the Reformed tradition is so much more than simply a footnote to him.

What we have attempted to do in this very small dictionary is provide a basic reference tool for folks who want to know a little about the people, movements and terms that are so important to the Reformed tradition. We view this resource, with just over three hundred entries, as a launching pad rather than a resting place. We hope to get you started in your appreciation of the tradition and to help remove the disorientation that so often occurs when entering a new conversation. We expect readers to dip in and out rather than read this book cover to cover. Instead of trying to give exhaustive definitions, we have provided short ones that give the newcomer sufficient background without overwhelming them, which is why most entries are only 75-150 words. In addition, rather than using more words to explain terms that appear elsewhere in the dictionary, we have used an asterisk to indicate each term that has an entry of its own, and we encourage readers to refer to those entries for further information and clarification.

We also invite the adventurous reader to use the extended bibliography provided at the end of this book. There we have offered suggestions for general introductions to the Reformed tradition, and we have also recommended samples of classic works from the early sixteenth century to our own day. These are meant to give a sense of the breadth and depth of the tradition. In this way the student can not only begin to read about the tradition but also explore the heart of the tradition through key primary sources. We hope this dictionary will help to facilitate this more intensive reading.

ACKNOWLEDGMENTS

We would like to thank a number of people who helped make this book possible.

I, Kelly, find intense joy in seeing former students use their gifts for Christ's kingdom. One of my great privileges in life is to work alongside them in scholarship, and this project allowed that to happen at multiple levels. I am particularly thankful that Wes was willing to work with me on this project, carrying a heavy share of the load and showing great ability not only with organizational detail but also in matters of style and substance. Proving to be not only an able theologian, Wes has also become a good friend, faithful with encouragement and prayer. This may be Wes's first book, but it certainly will not be his last, and for that I thank God. In many ways this book was a community project. I am thankful to Covenant College for their support of this project. In particular, former students of mine Cameron Moran, Heather Greenlee McGibbon, Justin Borger, Brian Hecker, Grady Dickinson and Jimmy Myers all helped at various levels with research and initial drafting of many entries, and this dictionary simply could not have been written without their contributions. Additionally, two of my colleagues graciously helped: William Tate provided invaluable feedback on the whole manuscript, and William Davis gave thoughtful suggestions on a fair number of difficult entries. We are deeply in debt to all who contributed. As always, I am thankful to my family, Tabitha, Jonathan and Margot, as each of you in your own way reminds me of the essence of faith that doesn't belittle scholarship but is also not dependent on it either. What a gift you three are to me. Lastly, I dedicate this book to Todd Capen and Jeff Weigum. Both men invested in me as a teenager and new believer. Under Todd's ministry I was converted, and he powerfully cultivated in me a passion for Christ, the joy of evangelism and a love for learning theology. And Jeff, as a volunteer, poured himself into the lives of Ben, Paul, Buster and me. While he may have never reached his educational goals, the result of his love and investment in us (none of us having grown up in the church) was that now, decades later, three of us have seminary degrees, two of us have PhDs and teach, one has done urban work directed toward those in need, and the fourth serves as a Navy Chaplain. What a testimony of kingdom service, love and grace. I thank them both for taking a teenager seriously and for introducing me to the basics of faith, hope and love.

I, Wes, am immensely grateful for the opportunity to work on this project, which arose through Kelly's gracious invitation. Beginning with the first class I took from Kelly more than ten years ago and continuing with the experience of working on this dictionary together, I have been inspired by his theological insight, encouraged by his personal example and thankful for his friendship. Kelly is the kind of theologian I long to be, someone who seeks an understanding of faith consistently working itself out in love and hope, and I look forward to more opportunities to learn from and work alongside him in the future. I would also like to thank Cameron Moran, Heather Greenlee McGibbon, Justin Borger, Brian Hecker, Grady Dickinson and Jimmy Myers for their invaluable assistance on many entries. I have appreciated their patient and gracious interaction regarding the details of particular entries, which are certainly more accurate and complete as a result of their effort. My wife, Stephanie, also made helpful comments on several entries, but I am most thankful for her constant encouragement and unfaltering support. She keeps my feet planted firmly on the ground, reminding me that the best theology impacts everyday life and builds up the church. Stephanie is God's greatest gift to me. And finally, I dedicate this book to my parents, because of whom I have always known Jesus. For them, the Reformed tradition is not merely a system of beliefs; it is a way of life. Through a variety of hardships and challenges, they have shown an unswerving commitment to the sovereignty of God and a passionate concern for his glory. I thank them for their example of faith that is rooted in Scripture, rich in doctrine, filled with wonder and curiosity in creation, and persistent in prayer. It is a joy to have parents who are also parents in the faith. May God continue to bless them and keep them.

A

accommodation. God's appropriation of humanly intelligible means to communicate real knowledge of himself. John *Calvin addressed the problem of how finite humans may obtain genuine *knowledge of God by emphasizing condescension as the distinctive manner of God's *revelation. God accommodates himself in creation, history and Scripture through and within the cultural and intellectual limits of humanity while effectively communicating truth and accomplishing his purposes. Some examples of God's accommodation include the images and anthropomorphic language describing God in Scripture and the way God relates to his creatures by making covenants and giving laws. The ultimate way God accommodates to humanity, however, is through the incarnation of Jesus Christ; in and through the Son's willing assumption of human weakness, God is able to accomplish our *salvation.

Acts of Uniformity. Edicts made by the English monarchy through Parliament to standardize *liturgy in the Church of England. The first (1548-1549) legally bound ministers to use the *Book of Common Prayer, and revised versions of the edicts required the use of subsequent editions of the Book of Common Prayer, whether under Edward VI (1551–1552), under Elizabeth I (1558–1559) or during the Restoration (1661–1662).

ad fontes. This Latin phrase meaning "to the fountain" or "to the sources" was used by *humanist scholars during the Renaissance, voicing their commitment to consult primary Greek and Latin sources in their efforts to improve modern society. Reformers employed this phrase as a call to engage directly with the Scriptures and early Christian texts in their original languages to ensure sound *doctrine within the church.

Alexander, Archibald (1772–1851). The first professor appointed at Princeton Theological Seminary at its founding in 1812. Along with Charles *Hodge and others, he helped establish what is now known as *Princeton Theology, adhering to the *Westminster Confession, arguing for the inerrancy of Scripture and advocating Scottish commonsense realism. Alexander contributed regularly to the *Princeton Review* and published many works of his own. A *Presbyterian pastor as well as a professor, he placed great emphasis on *piety and personal religious experience.

Ames, William (1576–1633). A leading English *Puritan theologian instrumental in the denunciation of the *Remonstrant beliefs at the Synod of *Dort. A student of William *Perkins at Cambridge, Ames applied the logic and philosophy of Peter Ramus to theology, viewing its primary task as classification and its goal as uncovering the mind of God. In 1610 he left Cambridge and made his way to the Netherlands where he began teaching at the University of Franeker in 1622, and his influence extended beyond Europe to North America. His best-known works are *The Marrow of Theology* and *Conscience with the Power and Cases Thereof.*

Anabaptism. Literally "re-baptism," the most general trait of this broad and decentralized *Protestant movement is the practice of *baptism for those who have experienced *conversion, even if they have been baptized as infants. This practice, together with insisting on the separation between the magistrate and the church, are two major distinctions between Anabaptists and the *magisterial Reformation. Beginning at the early stages of the *Swiss Reformation, various groups began to form what would become the *radical Reformation. Coming into conflict with the established church and civil authorities, whether Roman Catholic or Protestant, these groups focused on fully realizing the *marks of the church as presented in the book of Acts. They stressed social equality and communal interpretation of Scripture, much like the *Bohemian Brethren, and opposed *clergy who they believed fostered intellectual elitism. As such, they were sometimes considered anti-intellectual and, at least initially, anti-patriarchal. Andreas *Karlstadt and Thomas *Müntzer involved the movement in the *Peasants' War, during which many Anabaptists were killed. The movement expanded through refugee communities in such places as Moravia and the Netherlands. The most important figure for those who identified with its nonviolent aspects was Menno *Simmons, who helped to establish the Dutch Anabaptists and laid the basis for Mennonite communities. The modern influence of Anabaptism is as diverse as its beginnings, ranging from the

Amish and Hutterites to numerous *Baptist denominations.

analogia entis. A Latin phrase meaning "analogy of being," the medieval principle of how human language, by principle of analogy, can also be applied to God. Two reasons are usually given to defend this principle: all created reality has been ordered by God to make this possible, and humans bear God's *image. This allows finite human minds to reason from the effect (creation) to the cause (the Creator) and to know the nature of God apart from his *special revelation. Some have argued that by identifying a metaphysical foundation linking human thought with God's thought, the principle provides a basis for *natural theology. Rejecting this metaphysical assertion, Karl *Barth favored an *analogia fidei* and emphasized the primacy of special revelation. Some, however, accuse Barth of inappropriately framing this debate in metaphysical terms rather than linguistic ones, as many medievals proposed.

analogia fidei. A Latin phrase meaning "analogy of faith," referring to the principle that any interpretation must be in accord with the teaching of the Scripture taken as a whole. Arising out of Reformed *scholasticism, this principle posits that difficult passages of Scripture should be understood in light of general concepts derived from Scripture (e.g., *covenant or *biblical theology). This goes beyond *analogia scripturae*: interpreting difficult passages with clear ones. Karl *Barth revised it further by opposing it to the *analogia entis.* He argued that since *revelation alone discloses a likeness between God and humanity, one cannot separate knowledge of God's being from God's act of revelation. Therefore, no proposition counts as *knowledge of God unless it is related to God as revealed in the *Word of God.

Anglicanism. The branch of *Protestantism associated with the Church of England, beginning with Henry VIII's Act of Supremacy (1534), which officially launched the *English Reformation. During the reign of Elizabeth I, ministers such as John Jewel and Richard Hooker wrote important defenses of the Church of England, forging a middle way between Catholicism and the continental Reformation. Through the *Acts of Uniformity, the *Book of Common Prayer* as crafted by Thomas *Cranmer emerged as the standard for public *worship and *liturgy and the *Thirty-Nine Articles gave definition to Anglican *doctrine. Today the Anglican Communion contains immense diversity and is now the third largest affiliation of Christian churches in the world.

antinomianism. The belief (from Latin, "against the law") that Christians are free from any obligation to the law because they have been set free by *faith in the gospel. This precise term arose in a debate between Johann Agricola, Philipp *Melanchthon and Martin *Luther regarding the place of the law in the Christian life. Although Luther was criticized for making light of the law through an emphasis on *sola fide and *sola gratia, he sought to settle the debate by writing *Against the Antinomians* (1539), asserting that *law and gospel are not opposed. Other Reformers, such as John *Calvin, affirmed the benefit of the law in its three uses, although debate about the law's continuing significance persisted after the *Reformation, as in the case of *Puritan Anne Hutchinson in seventeenth-century New England.

apologetics. The theory and practice of defending Christianity. Numerous apologetic tasks are recognized within the Reformed tradition, including answering objections, responding to heterodoxy, demonstrating rational coherence of theological systems, providing evidence for the faith, assuaging doubts and exploring presuppositions. At the heart of the tradition, however, is the conviction held by theologians such as *Calvin and *Barth that God's triune *revelation, rather than human reason, is the final arbiter in apologetic arguments. Reformed methods include classical, philosophical, *presuppositional and *worldview apologetics as advocated by (among others) B. B. *Warfield, Herman *Dooyeweerd, Cornelius *Van Til and Francis *Schaeffer, respectively.

apostasy. Intentional abandonment and rejection of *faith previously professed. *Reformed theology takes biblical warnings against apostasy seriously, seeing them as a means by which God commands and empowers his people to persevere with faithful obedience. The possibility of true and total apostasy, therefore, is not viewed as contrary to the *perseverance of the saints; rather, apostasy is a real phenomenon when those who have merely professed faith outwardly and have participated in the visible *church then reject the faith either in word or in deed, making internal realities publicly known.

architecture, church. Medieval church buildings incorporated a complex system of theologically significant structures and images, an approach challenged by many sixteenth-century Reformers. *Luther argued that true *worship does not need a building, and other Reformers such as *Calvin and *Zwingli agreed that a simple meeting hall was sufficient for Christian worship. Many early Protestant congregations, however, worshiped in formerly Roman Catholic church buildings, often moving the pulpit to a more central location as well as removing statues of saints and stained glass images. The growth of *Protestantism in the early seventeenth century was accompanied by the construction of new Protestant churches, ranging in style from simple rural buildings to the extravagant baroque structures of English architect Christopher Wren.

Arminianism. A theological system based on the teachings of Dutch theologian Jacobus *Arminius and his early followers, the *Remonstrants. After Arminius's death, the Remonstrants issued five articles summarizing their beliefs in opposition to *Calvinists, who countered with the Canons of *Dort, much later summarized by *TULIP. While originally condemned as heretics by the Synod of Dort, the Remonstrants later obtained legal toleration in Holland, and many Protestants still adhere to Arminianism today. While it has many *doctrines in common with *Reformed theology, it differs significantly in its teaching on *predestination, *free will and *atonement. The system follows Arminius's original teachings that God's *election is conditional on his *foreknowledge of human free choice, that God provides *prevenient grace to everyone in order to enable people to choose *faith in Jesus, and that believers are able to lose their *salvation since they always have the free will to accept or reject Christ. Contemporary Arminianism includes a wide variety of viewpoints on key issues, like whether the governmental or penal-substitutionary atonement is more accurate. Arminians today also differ at times with Arminius's own views, such as his support of infant *baptism, which is now opposed by most Arminians.

Arminius, Jacobus (1560–1609). The Latinized name of Dutch theologian, pastor and writer Jakob Hermanszoon. He is most remembered for his views on *predestination, *free will, *grace, *atonement and *perseverance of the saints, which differed from the traditional *Augustinian and *Calvinist doctrines as expressed in the *Belgic Confession and *Heidelberg Catechism. Arminius was educated at Marburg (1575), Leiden (1576–1581), Basel (1582–1583) and Geneva (1582, 1584–1586), and studied under *Calvin's successor, Theodore *Beza. He served as a pastor in Amsterdam from 1588 to 1603 and as professor of theology at the University of Leiden from 1603 to the end of his life. Arminius came to oppose unconditional *election and *supralapsarianism, arguing instead that God's election was conditional on his *foreknowledge of who would choose *faith in Christ. He also taught that Christ accomplished a universal *atonement, although only those who believe in Christ are saved. He maintained that the Holy Spirit provides *prevenient grace enabling humans to believe in Christ, but that people can fall away from *salvation because of their free will. After his death, the *Remonstrants proposed five articles challenging *Calvinism, resulting in the Canons of *Dort, which later have been associated with *TULIP. Those who subscribed to Arminius's views became known as Arminians, though the theology of contemporary *Arminianism differs in some ways from his original teachings.

assurance of salvation (assurance of faith). Confidence regarding the power and promise of God to accomplish *salvation, which follows from other Reformed *doctrines of grace, such as *election and *perseverance of the saints. Some Reformers, such as John *Calvin, were careful to distinguish between objective assurance as a gift of the Holy Spirit and subjective or psychological certainty, recognizing the presence of doubt and anxiety in the Christian life. Others argued for absolute certainty as a sign of true *faith, motivating the *Council of Trent to criticize the "ungodly confidence" of this position. In *A Treatise Concerning Religious Affections* (1746), Jonathan *Edwards argued that although there is no infallible sign of election, *holiness is the chief mark of true religion (i.e., *regeneration).

atonement. Describing the reconciliation of God and humanity, this *doctrine identifies the agent and means of *salvation with the work of Christ culminating at the cross. Reformed accounts typically use the structure of the covenant to describe God as the agent and Christ as the instrument of reconciliation, also emphasizing the primacy of Christ's mediation (*solus Christus*), the judicial imagery of satisfaction (*propitiation) and *union with Christ. Normally the emphasis is on the finished work of Christ in his atoning sacrifice, his death on the cross exhaustively overcoming the guilt and threat of *sin. Theologians like John *Calvin and Karl *Barth highlighted the judicial aspect of God's *election and Christ's atonement. Against the trend of limiting the cross to a mere moral example, Reformed theologians as diverse as Friedrich *Schleiermacher and Thomas *Torrance accentuated the power of Christ's death to accomplish redemption and reconciliation.

Auburn Avenue Theology. *See* federal vision.

Augsburg Confession (1530). Written primarily by Philipp *Melanchthon, this *confession of faith is one of the earliest *Lutheran summaries of belief. Its twenty-eight articles were later included in the *Book of Concord*. The first twenty-one articles address *doctrines about God, Christ, *sin, *justification, the church and its ministry, Christian behavior, and *eschatology, while the remaining seven address ecclesiastical abuses to be amended.

Augustinianism. A theological tradition based on the vast influence of St. Augustine of Hippo (354–430). Augustine's legacy includes his intimate autobiographical musings in the *Confessions*, leadership as a bishop in North Africa during the Donatist controversy (a conflict over the validity of *sacraments performed by ministers who had repudiated their faith during persecution), reflection on the church and the state in *The City of God*, a seminal treatise on *trinitarian theology, and many biblical commentaries. Throughout his works, Augustine observes the enslaving nature of *sin and thus humanity's need for divine *grace in contrast to the emphasis on human *free will as expounded in *Pelagianism. *Luther, *Calvin and the other Reformers not only appealed to Augustine in articulating their own theology but also viewed the *Reformation as a rediscovery of the *doctrines of grace that Augustine had championed during his battle with Pelagius. Luther made special use of Augustine's emphasis on *total depravity in debates with *Erasmus, while Calvin took particular interest in developing his insights into *predestination. In addition, Jonathan *Edwards celebrated Augustine's effective use of rhetoric as well as the aesthetic quality of his theology. Overall, Reformed theologians typically draw more heavily from Augustine's anthropology, his view of *original sin, and his emphasis on the relationship between divine *sovereignty and *grace, rather than drawing from his *ecclesiology. As B. B. *Warfield memorably claimed in his essay titled "Augustine," "The Reformation, inwardly considered, was just the ultimate triumph of Augustine's doctrine of grace over Augustine's doctrine of the Church." Even though the principle of *sola scriptura freed Reformed theologians to critique Augustine's theology at times, the Reformed tradition, which has always been thoroughly Augustinian, owes a great debt to the Bishop of Hippo.

B

Babylonian Captivity. This phrase, which alludes to the kingdom of Judah's seventy years of captivity in ancient Babylon, was memorably used to refer to the period between 1309 and 1377 when the *papacy resided in Avignon, France, for political reasons before returning to Rome. The phrase should not be confused with the title of Martin *Luther's treatise, *On the Babylonian Captivity of the Church*, which criticized the Roman Catholic Church's "captivity" to a corrupt papacy and sacramental system.

baptism. The *sacrament of initiation using water, either by sprinkling or immersing the recipient, to symbolize *regeneration by the Holy Spirit through *union with Christ in his death and resurrection. Jesus gave his disciples the authority to baptize as an integral part of their *mission, and together with the *Lord's Supper, Protestants consider baptism a sacrament because it was directly commanded by Christ. Performed in the name of the Father, Son and Holy Spirit, it is intrinsically connected to *trinitarian theology, which is also evident in the form of catechesis that often precedes (for adults) or follows (for infants) baptism. While retaining this pedagogical focus, all Protestant churches removed the exorcism and anointing that are performed in the classic Roman Catholic rite. John *Calvin gave baptism a central place in the Sunday *liturgy and prefaced it with *preaching in order to emphasize its function as an outward sign of the inward reality of *salvation *sola gratia. As an application of God's promise to one unable to speak, Calvin considered infant baptism to be a powerful sign of the primacy of *grace. With Martin *Luther and Ulrich *Zwingli, he defended infant baptism by citing Jesus' blessing of the children in the Gospels and the circumcision of infants in the old covenant. In line with *Augustinianism, the Reformers considered the worthiness of the minister or recipient independent of the sacrament's effectiveness and condemned rebaptism. *Anabaptists, however, rejected infant baptism and commended rebaptism of confessing adults. Some in the Reformed tradition, such as Reformed *Baptists, follow in this tradition and continue to promote adult or believer's baptism.

Baptists, Reformed. Also commonly known as Calvinist Baptists or Particular Baptists, this group traces its roots back to the Separatist movement in late sixteenth-century and early seventeenth-century England. Most Reformed Baptist churches today still adhere to the 1689 London Baptist Confession of Faith composed by Particular Baptists, so named because they differed from the General Baptists in affirming that Christ's *atonement applies particularly to the elect. Reformed Baptists hold to the five *solas* of the *Reformation (*sola fide, *sola gratia, *sola scriptura, *soli deo gloria, *solus Christus) and share a view of God's *sovereignty and *soteriology similar to that affirmed by other Reformed traditions. While upholding believer's *baptism (commonly requiring immersion), they reject paedobaptism (i.e., the baptism of infants).

Barmen Declaration (1934). A statement of belief produced by the Confessing Church in Barmen, Germany, under the leadership of Karl *Barth, which resisted the theological aberrations and increased allegiance to the Reich government within the German Evangelical Church by asserting the lordship of Jesus Christ as the *Word of God and the distinct roles of church and state.

Barth, Karl (1886–1968). Influential Swiss theologian and leader of *dialectical theology, known for, among other things, his opposition to liberalism, his emphatic Christocentrism and his fresh approach to *revelation. He began his career as a pastor, serving the Swiss community of Safenwil (1911–1921). During this period, his attitude toward the Protestant liberal heritage of Friedrich *Schleiermacher in which he was trained changed dramatically. In 1914, he broke with his old teachers over their political support for the kaiser in World War I. Furthermore, finding liberal theology inadequate to meet the demands of ministry, his study of the Bible culminated in his 1918 Romans commentary. Following the book's sensational reception, Barth's academic career began with his appointment as professor of Reformed theology at Göttingen. Appointments to Münster and Bonn followed, and his theology matured. During this time, he worked with several other theologians, including Emil *Brunner, to produce the periodical *Between the Times* (1922–1933), which marked the beginning of *dialectical theology. The group eventually dissolved due to growing differences over cultural events in Germany and Barth's rejection of *natural theology. Barth's political involvement in Germany increased, and in 1934 he was the principle author of the *Barmen Declaration. After being expelled from Bonn in the following year for failing to take an oath to Hitler, he returned to his native Basel and taught at the university for the remainder of his career. He had begun his multivolume magnum opus *Church Dogmatics* in 1932, which is driven by a christological focus, the priority of God's freedom, a distinct view of *election and the importance of *analogia fidei*. This work consumed his remaining career and was left unfinished, though it remains highly influential and has caused some to consider Barth one of the most important theologians in the past 250 years.

Basel Confession (1534). Completed by Oswald Myconius in 1532 and adopted by the Basel city council in 1534, this brief confession was based on an earlier draft by Johannes Oecolampadius. Supported by Martin *Bucer, it affirmed basic tenets of Protestant belief and attempted to mediate the positions of *Luther and *Zwingli regarding the *Lord's Supper.

Bavinck, Herman (1854–1921). A Dutch pastor and theologian contributing to the revival of *Reformed theology in the Dutch Reformed Church. After pastoring two years in Franeker, Bavinck taught *systematic theology at the Theological Seminary in Kampen and later the Free University of Amsterdam, where he succeeded Abraham *Kuyper. His four-volume *Reformed Dogmatics* was his most influential publication. The work upholds the primacy of Scripture while critically and sympathetically engaging with philosophical and social issues. Despite his disagreements with Kuyper, Bavinck shared Kuyper's passion for a world-encompassing Christianity and the relevance of theology to all of life.

Baxter, Richard (1615–1691). A prolific writer and English *Puritan pastor. Baxter served the handloom worker community for nearly twenty years in Kidderminster, where he preached as "a dying man to dying men." Predominantly self-educated, he was converted through his own private reading of the Scripture. After serving as a chaplain for a short period in Cromwell's army and recovering from an illness, Baxter returned to Kidderminster to focus on writing. Some of his nearly two hundred works include *The Saints' Everlasting Rest* (1650), a much loved devotional work he wrote during serious illness; *The Reformed Pastor* (1656), combating patterns of pastoral neglect; and some polemical works, such as his controversial treatise on *justification.

Belgic Confession (1561). Originally written in French (1561) by Guido de Brès, this confession in Dutch translation (1562) became a doctrinal standard of the Reformed tradition, originally adopted by the Reformed Church of the Netherlands (Antwerp, 1566). Like the *French Confession, an appeal for tolerance sent to King Philip II of Spain was the base text for this confession.

Belhar Confession (1982). A declaration written in Afrikaans by theologians of the Dutch Reformed Mission Church in South Africa, this confession opposed apartheid and identifies unity, reconciliation and *social justice as central to the gospel. After it was adopted by the Uniting Reformed Church in Southern Africa, other denominations, such as the Reformed Church in America, adopted it as a confessional standard.

Berkhof, Hendrikus (1914–1995). A Dutch Reformed theologian, Berkhof served as a pastor and later the director of the Reformed Church seminary in Driebergen. In 1960, he was appointed professor of *dogmatic and *biblical theology at the University of Leiden, and during his twenty-one years of teaching, he sought a middle way between "rigid traditionalism" and "rudderless modernism." Influenced by Karl *Barth, Berkhof departed from Barth's methodology particularly in advocating contextual *Christology, articulated most definitively along with other *doctrines in Berkhof's *Christian Faith* (1979, revised 1986).

Berkhof, Louis (1873–1957). A Dutch-American Reformed theologian. Berkhof was born in the Netherlands but moved to the United States as a child. He studied for several years under B. B. *Warfield and Geerhardus *Vos at Princeton Seminary and was ordained in the Christian Reformed Church. After several years of pastoral experience, he taught biblical studies and *systematic theology at Calvin Theological Seminary, later serving there as president until his retirement in 1944. His most influential academic work was *Systematic Theology* (1938), which drew heavily from Reformed *scholasticism; it became a widely accepted and utilized summary of *Reformed theology.

Berkouwer, Gerrit Cornelis (1903–1996). A theologian and ecumenical church leader within the Reformed Churches in the Netherlands (GKN). Influenced by both Abraham *Kuyper and Herman *Bavinck, Berkouwer navigated the contemporary maze of liberalism, neo-orthodoxy and *scholasticism through his lectures as professor of *systematic theology at the Free University of Amsterdam. In addition to publishing eighteen volumes of *Studies in Dogmatics* (translated into fourteen English volumes), Berkouwer produced a sympathetic yet critical evaluation of Karl *Barth's theology and several volumes on Roman Catholic theology, confirming his expertise in ecumenical dialogue.

Beza, Theodore (1519–1605). A French Calvinist theologian who was a colleague and successor to *Calvin both in Geneva and within the Reformed movement as a whole. Originally a *humanist in the Roman Catholic Church, Beza began reading Reformed literature and eventually fled to Geneva in 1548. Finding no work there, he taught Greek in Lausanne until 1558, when *Calvin offered Beza a position at the newly founded Geneva Academy. After Calvin's death in 1564, Beza became the effective leader of the Reformed church in Geneva, handling disputes with *Lutheranism, particularly regarding the *Lord's Supper. Although in general Beza aligned theologically with Calvin, he did modify and develop some particular *doctrines, such as *supralapsarian *predestination, and his concern for doctrinal details laid the groundwork for the growth of Reformed *scholasticism.

biblical theology. This practice of discerning the theological testimony, unity and development of the biblical *canon was a concern of the Reformers, but it began to emerge as an approach distinct from *dogmatic theology in the seventeenth and eighteenth centuries. Having much in common with *covenant theology, Reformed approaches usually emphasize the unity of Scripture as a *redemptive-historical drama, all of which reveals the person and work of Christ. Notable Reformed theologians who developed a distinctive methodological approach known as biblical theology in more recent history include Adolf *Schlatter, Geerhardus *Vos and Herman *Ridderbos, and most contemporary scholars appreciate how this discipline complements and integrates with *systematic theology.

Bloesch, Donald G. (1928–2010). An American theologian raised in the *pietist tradition who demonstrated a vital engagement with contextual and *biblical theology. A professor at the University of Dubuque Theological Seminary for thirty-five years, he initially wrote on the renewal of evangelical theology and, more particularly, spiritual renewal within the United Church of Christ. Deeply influenced by *Barth and *Brunner, he emphasized in his mature, seven-volume *Christian Foundations* that God's action is the foundation for the dynamic interplay between subjective *faith and objective *revelation. He argued, for example, against identifying revelation with the literal propositions of the biblical text or reducing exegesis to historical study.

Bohemian Brethren. This pre-Reformation movement was inspired by Jan *Hus and called for participation of laity in the *Lord's Supper and interpretation of Scripture by the community. Emerging as a movement in the mid-fifteenth century and with ties to the *Waldensians, the Brethren promoted an ideal of rural and communal life and were further influenced by *Calvinism in the sixteenth century. While making important contributions to the Czech language, especially with a Bible *translation (1579–1593), the Brethren suffered persecution and established several émigré communities, particularly in Poland. After suppression in the seventeenth century, a remnant joined the Lutheran *pietists at Herrnhut (1721) and were absorbed into the Moravian Church.

bondage of the will. A phrase originating from the title of a book written in 1525 by Martin *Luther (originally in Latin, *De Servo Arbitrio*), responding to *Erasmus's treatise on *free will. Luther argued that Erasmus misconstrued Scripture by defending unobstructed free will, claiming instead that without the liberating *grace of the Holy Spirit, the human will is enslaved to *sin and at enmity against God. Instead, *salvation is entirely dependent on God's will and mercy, a foundational tenet of *Reformed theology.

Bonhoeffer, Dietrich (1906–1945). A German Lutheran pastor and theologian. After extensive theological training in Germany and America, Bonhoeffer worked as a chaplain and lecturer in *systematic theology at the University of Berlin during Hitler's rise to power. Along with Karl *Barth, whose theology had a lasting impact on Bonhoeffer, he signed the *Barmen Declaration in 1934 in opposition to the Reich *government. After short stints as a pastor in London and as a professor at Union Theological Seminary in New York, he returned to Germany and became involved in Reich resistance. As a result, Bonhoeffer was arrested and, two years later, executed at the age of thirty-nine. Although a Lutheran, Bonhoeffer's theological works share many features with *Reformed theology, and his more practical works, such as *The Cost of Discipleship* and *Life Together*, have wielded enormous influence within *evangelicalism.

Book of Common Order. The official guide for worship and other services within Scottish *Presbyterianism. While in Geneva,

John *Knox and others crafted the *Genevan Book of Order* for use by the English congregation, which was later the basis for the official *Book of Common Order* by the Church of Scotland in 1562, containing orders for corporate *worship, the *sacraments, *prayer, *marriages, funerals, *ordination and other services. In 1645, the *Directory for Public Worship*, which resulted from the *Westminster Assembly, was adopted with slight variation by the General Assembly in Scotland to replace the *Book of Common Order*. Every subsequent development of Presbyterianism used these books as templates for their own directories, often called the *Book of Church Order* or simply the *Book of Order*.

Book of Common Prayer (1549). The official worship guide for the Church of England, originally assembled by Thomas *Cranmer to reform medieval *liturgy during the reign of the Protestant King Edward VI as part of the *Acts of Uniformity, containing "daily office" (scheduled readings and prayers), forms for administering *sacraments, other rites and ceremonies, and the Psalter.

Book of Concord (1580). This compendium of seven documents central to *Lutheranism republished the *Augsburg Confession on the fiftieth anniversary of its presentation to Charles V and included *Luther's two *catechisms and the *Schmalkaldic Articles. While intended to be ecumenical and normative, its reception has been mixed as the authoritative statement of Lutheran orthodoxy, although it remains central for distinguishing Lutheranism from *Reformed theology.

Bora, Katharina von (1499–1552). A German nun who later became the wife of Martin *Luther. Bora left her life as a nun and fled to Wittenberg after she became convinced of the theology being taught by Luther and other Reformers. She married Luther in 1525 and became actively involved in his ministry and helped to provide for them financially by managing their household, farm, brewery and other properties. As the wife of such a prominent theologian, she helped promote a positive view of Protestant family life. Together they had six children, four of whom survived to adulthood.

Boston, Thomas (1676–1732). A Church of Scotland minister and theologian best known for his contributions to *covenant theology and his involvement in the Marrow Controversy in the Church of Scotland. Boston's role in the Marrow Controversy involved opposing a legalistic strain in the Church of Scotland with a robust theology of *grace. His most famous published work, *Human Nature in Its Fourfold State,* remains in print. Boston is also remembered for his study of divine inspiration and his two-covenant view—a covenant of works and a covenant of grace—in contrast with the three-covenant view articulated earlier by Johannes *Cocceius.

Brakel, Wilhelmus à (1635–1711). A Dutch theologian and pastor. Wilhelmus à Brakel was born to a pastor near Leeuwarden in the Netherlands. Attending the Academy at Franeker, Wilhelmus was ordained to be a minister in 1659, serving various churches in the northern Netherlands for fifty years. Near the end of his life, he wrote *The Christian's Reasonable Service,* a popular and influential multivolume treatise offering a unique blend of robust theology and pastoral concern. Through his ministry and writing he is remembered as a leading representative of the *Dutch Second Reformation (*Nadere Reformatie*).

Brunner, Heinrich Emil (1889–1966). A Swiss theologian who, along with Karl *Barth, opposed the hegemonic liberal theology in Europe with neo-orthodox and *dialectical theology. Brunner was a professor of *systematic and practical theology at the University of Zurich and a visiting lecturer at leading universities around the world. Despite their similar theological commitments, Brunner clashed with Barth over the issue of *natural theology, claiming that God's *revelation extends beyond the person of Jesus Christ. Like Barth, Brunner published widely, most notably a three-volume *Dogmatics* summarizing his approach to *Reformed theology and also reflecting his characteristic ecumenical concerns.

Bucer, Martin (1491–1551). A Protestant Reformer from South Germany. Bucer joined the *Reformation through the influence of Martin *Luther, leaving the Dominican order. After moving to Strasbourg, Bucer became an important leader who sought to resolve the controversies between the Swiss Reformed and Lutherans regarding the *Lord's Supper, eventually reaching an agreement with Philipp *Melanchthon. Upon his exile to

Britain, Bucer became a professor at Cambridge and assisted
Edward VI's reform of the church, his influence notable in the
Book of Common Prayer.

Bullinger, Heinrich (1504–1575). A leading Swiss Reformer who
was appointed successor to Ulrich *Zwingli in 1531. He was the
primary author of the First and Second *Helvetic Confession,
and noted for seeking unity among Reformed leaders on the
*Lord's Supper. Reading the church fathers, *Luther and *Mel-
anchthon at Cologne (1519–1522), he became committed to the
Reformation. After becoming head teacher at the Cistercian
monastery at Kappel in early 1523, he helped advance reform
and wrote numerous biblical commentaries. In 1529, he was
appointed pastor of his hometown in Bremgarten but fled to
Zurich, where he remained until his death.

Bunyan, John (1628–1688). An English *Puritan preacher and
writer during the Restoration of the English monarchy and
the Anglican church. During an imprisonment for *preaching
without a license, Bunyan wrote his best-known work, *Pilgrim's
Progress,* a Christian allegory that served as an accessible and
popular introduction to a Puritan approach to the Christian
life. In addition to *Pilgrim's Progress,* he published over sixty
books, including a spiritual autobiography, *Grace Abounding to
the Chief of Sinners.* The popularity of the works of this *Baptist
preacher, both in Great Britain and the American colonies, was
instrumental in the spread of *Calvinist and Puritan theology.

Buswell, J. Oliver (1895–1977). American theologian, pastor
and professor who was instrumental in founding the Orthodox
Presbyterian Church (1936) and the Bible Presbyterian Church
(1937). During his career, Buswell, who served as president of
Wheaton College (Illinois) and later as dean of Covenant Theological Seminary, was widely known for his *Systematic Theology of the Christian Religion.* Due to his stalwart *fundamentalist
beliefs, Buswell often found himself at odds with other Reformed theologians of his day over his support of abstinence
from alcohol and the *dispensationalist *Scofield Reference Bible.*
He remains widely respected, however, for his commitment to
Reformed principles and his faithful leadership within American *Presbyterianism.

C

Calvin, John (1509–1564). Born in Noyon, France, Calvin received a *humanist education in law at Paris, Orléans and Bourges, where he was influenced by the *devotio moderna,* which emphasized *piety and spiritual revival within the church. Calvin studied the writings of Desiderius *Erasmus, Martin *Luther and others, but left Paris for Basel to escape the Inquisition. There he became involved with the *Swiss Reformation and published the first edition of the *Institutes of the Christian Religion* in Latin (1536), which established his voice as a second-generation Reformer. While he intended to study with Martin *Bucer in Strasbourg, William *Farel persuaded him to help establish reform in Geneva. As their work commenced, a disagreement with the city council in 1538 led to both Farel's and Calvin's expulsion. This provided the opportunity for Calvin to accept Bucer's invitation to work in Strasbourg. During this time, Calvin preached, lectured and took part in numerous religious dialogues, which resulted in the second edition of the *Institutes* (1539), now in French, and his Romans commentary (1539). When Cardinal Sadoleto urged the Genevan church to return to *papacy, the Genevan city council asked Calvin to respond on their behalf and to return in 1541. Calvin would remain there for the rest of his life.

As a member of the *magisterial Reformation, Calvin used his legal and theological training to shape the reform of Geneva around biblical principles. Toward that end, he wrote the *Geneva Catechism and a new *liturgy, and he kept revising the *Institutes* until its fourth and definitive edition in 1559, which together with his biblical commentaries shaped the identity of Reformed *orthodoxy beyond the influence of Ulrich *Zwingli. Following the principle of *sola scriptura,* Calvin determined that *systematic theology must express the truth of the *Word of God with brevity and clarity for the sake of *piety. While he agreed with Martin *Luther's understanding of *justification by faith, Calvin disagreed with his understanding of *law and gospel; instead, Calvin proposed a new way forward by employing a rich *pneumatology that placed God's grace at the center of *sanctification. In addition to his commitment to his theological writing, Calvin preached as many as two hundred times a year. He organized regular meetings of local pastors, promoting Bible study as well as mentoring and mutual correction, and encouraging the proper functions of the four church *offices. In 1553, Calvin allowed the Spanish theologian and scientist Michael Servetus, who taught modalism, to burn to death for his heterodox *trinitarian theology. Other Swiss Reformed congregations and Philipp *Melanchthon approved this decision.

Calvin's work of reform extended beyond the city through his constant correspondence with numerous leaders throughout Europe and Britain. In 1541, he signed the *Augsburg Confession, written by Melanchthon, and contributed to the Zurich Consensus in 1549, which represented a synthesis of his own view of the *Lord's Supper with the *memorialism of Heinrich *Bullinger by positing the *real presence of Christ during the Lord's Supper through the work of the Holy Spirit. Geneva served as a base for the reform movement in France, a mission dear to Calvin's heart, served greatly by his French *Institutes* and catechism. His appeal to the French King Henri II for tolerance served as the basis for the *French Confession. In 1559, the Geneva Academy was founded, and through it Calvin influenced numerous future Reformers, including John *Knox. His successor in this effort was Theodore *Beza, who laid the groundwork for Reformed *scholasticism and *Calvinism. When Calvin died after a painful illness, his final wish was to be buried with a simple ceremony and without a marker, which was a reflection of his *iconoclasm and his aversion to the cult of the *saints, but also a fitting final message from one whose prophetic voice sought to call God's people to attend to God's Word. Calvin's enduring legacy is clearly seen in how this call to attend to God's *revelation has influenced the very core of modern theology as exhibited in the work of such diverse theologians as Friedrich *Schleiermacher, Herman *Bavinck, Karl *Barth and J. I. *Packer.

Calvinism. As a synonym for the Reformed tradition, this term highlights the influence of John *Calvin and his work in Geneva in shaping the movement. While Calvin did wield considerable influence, Calvinism is a complex tradition shaped in its early stages by many leaders, including Ulrich *Zwingli, William *Farel, Heinrich *Bullinger, Martin *Bucer and John *Knox. Calvin himself was interested in reconciling with *Lutheranism, which shared similar concerns for *sola scriptura, *justification by faith, rejection of a corrupt and theologically errant *papacy, and the *marks of the true church. By the mid-sixteenth century, however, differences had solidified, and the Reformed or Calvinist perspective was demarcated by a commitment to the comprehensive *sovereignty of God, a view of the *Lord's Supper distinct from *Lutheranism, an emphasis on the positive third use of the *law and a distinct practice of church *polity. It is difficult to generalize, however, because as the theology and cultural system of Calvinism spread from Switzerland to France, the Netherlands, Scotland, Ireland, England, Hungary and eventually North America, it continued to develop and adapt to particular localities, controversies and personalities. The Canons of *Dort were a benchmark for distinguishing the movement from *Arminianism, although numerous *confessions of faith had previously outlined Calvinist belief and practice. Consequently, while some identify *TULIP as an accurate summary of the *five points of Calvinism, these *doctrines alone actually limit, and in some cases even caricature and misrepresent, the complexity and breadth of the tradition.

Cameronians. Named for their identification with Richard Cameron, the "lion of the covenant" (1648–1680), these zealous *Covenanters sought to establish *Presbyterianism as the only valid form of religion in Scotland. Opposing the Roman Catholic monarchs Charles II and James II (James VII of Scotland), they were persecuted and occasionally martyred. They raised a regiment in support of William of Orange during the Glorious Revolution, and dissatisfied with the resulting religious settlement, they distanced themselves from other Covenanters and the Church of Scotland by forming a particular church, the Reformed Presbyterian, in 1743. While some congregations remain, the majority united with the Free Church of Scotland in 1876.

canon, biblical. Meaning biblical standard or rule, this is the list of books the church recognizes to be the written *Word of God. Until the *Council of Trent, the list was divided into those books universally accepted by the *tradition and those, including the Old Testament Apocrypha and several minor non-Pauline New Testament letters, whose authority was questioned by the church fathers. The *French, *Belgic, *Scots and Second *Helvetic Confessions and the *Thirty-Nine Articles gave every canonical book equal authority while rejecting the canonical status of the Apocrypha. They also underlined the preeminence of God's formation of the canon in order to criticize the Roman Catholic emphasis upon the church's role in determining the list.

catechism. Named after *katēcheō*, the Greek verb for oral instruction, this is a summary of Christian *doctrine used for religious instruction, presented in question-and-answer form. Although the practice is much older, this particular word and its distinctive form were first popularized during the Reformation by Martin *Luther. The intention was to present a distinctive, dialogical interpretation of the Nicene Creed, the Decalogue, the Lord's Prayer, the *sacraments and other doctrinal topics. A smaller, or shorter, catechism is usually intended for memorization by children, while a larger catechism is for more advanced study and often aimed at parents and church leaders. The most important Reformed examples are the *Geneva Catechism, the *Heidelberg Catechism, and the Westminster Shorter and Larger Catechisms, with the latter based on the *Westminster Confession instead of the Nicene Creed.

cause, primary and secondary. A classic philosophical principle distinguishing between the primary agency of a noncontingent, infinite being and the secondary agency of contingent, finite beings. Reformed *scholasticism, growing out of medieval scholasticism, carefully developed this distinction to explain how all things live, move and have their being in God, and yet how God is not the author of evil nor does he manipulate his creation like a puppeteer. For example, *Bavinck represents the tradition when he observes that while "wood burns and it is God alone who makes it burn," this process of burning should not formally be attributed to God but to the wood, which serves as the subject. Similarly, while people are the ones who believe, act and speak, only God can supply the sinner "all the vitality and strength he or she needs for the commission of sin." Yet, it is the sinner, not God, who is the subject/author of the sin (cf. *Westminster Confession of Faith 3.1). Relating God's infinite will and *decree to the *free will of creatures in this way has shaped Reformed perspectives on many issues, including the *providence of God, *compatibilism and *prayer. Furthermore, following Aquinas, miracles are often defined as God exercising his supernatural work without the use of normal secondary causes.

Chalmers, Thomas (1780–1847). Scottish minister, theologian and social visionary. Chalmers's career began as a minister in rural Scotland, where he developed his passion for parish *education, *preaching and relief for the poor. He tested these commitments in the parish of St. John's in urban Glasgow, where his influence spread because of the social vision articulated in *The Christian and Civic Economy of Large Towns.* Chalmers went on to hold professorships at the University of St Andrews (1823–1828) and the University of Edinburgh (1828–1843), teaching and writing on moral philosophy and *natural theology. As an evangelical leader within the Church of Scotland, Chalmers led the Disruption of 1843 and the formation of the Free Church of Scotland over the issues of patronage and the spiritual jurisdiction of the church.

Christ and culture. The title of a 1951 book by H. Richard *Niebuhr and a phrase used subsequently to describe the relationship between Christianity and the cultures in which it is situated. Originally, Niebuhr suggested five possible paradigms for this relationship: Christ against culture (as practiced, for example, by the Amish), Christ of culture (common among mainline churches), Christ above culture (the traditional Roman Catholic approach), Christ and culture in paradox (endorsed by many Lutherans), and Christ the transformer of culture. Niebuhr situated *Calvinism within this last motif, although he has been criticized for being overly simplistic, especially since perspectives vary within the Reformed tradition regarding the most faithful posture toward culture. On the one hand, the *two-kingdoms view often identifies the church as specifically relevant to sacred matters and is hesitant about the church addressing broadly "secular" or cultural concerns or exercising political power; on the other hand, *neo-Calvinism interprets every sphere of culture as a manifestation of God's created order and an arena of God's redemptive activity, despite how each sphere is distorted by *sin. While both ends of the spectrum value *vocational calling, the latter tends to emphasize *social action, holistic *mission, *common grace and the possibility of cultural renewal or transformation, whereas the former highlights the *spirituality of the church, the mission of *Word and *sacrament, God's special *grace to his people, and their responsibility to remain distinct from the surrounding culture. Perspectives on this issue are connected to a constellation of related topics, including the relationship between *law and gospel, the purpose of *education, the possibility of *natural theology, the extent of *pneumatology, and the nature of Christian *piety.

Christology. This central locus of *systematic theology covers the person and work of Christ; confessing Jesus Christ as both God and man, the church then also holds to the saving significance of his life, death, resurrection and ascension. Protestants follow *tradition by interpreting Scripture through the lens of the Chalcedonian formula: the perfect union in one person of the divine and human natures of Christ. Like their orthodox *trinitarian theology, the Reformers retained this *doctrine received from tradition while maintaining a concern for *sola scriptura, articulating their beliefs about Jesus according to the witness of the biblical *canon. Martin *Luther declared that Christ's suffering on the cross is where God is revealed as "for us," and he identified all right theological reflection as a *theologia crucis as opposed to *theologia gloriae. John *Calvin interpreted Christ as the *Word of God, relying especially on Johannine theology, and articulated what would become Reformed *orthodoxy's distinction between the divine and human aspects of Christ's work. Although it is part of ancient tradition, *Lutherans, who favor the *ubiquity of Christ, derisively call this distinction in Christ's work the *extra calvinisticum. Modern Reformed treatments, such as those by Friedrich *Schleiermacher and Karl *Barth, interweave the identity of Christ's person with *soteriology, often proceeding along the lines of the hymn in Philippians 2, where the disclosure of Christ's person comes through God's vindication of Christ's self-emptying sacrifice.

church discipline. One of the three *marks of the church as outlined in later Reformed *confessions. Church discipline refers to the regulation of Christian conduct by appointed leaders. The Reformer Ulrich *Zwingli maintained that magistrates held responsibility for discipline in both civil and ecclesial spheres, whereas later Reformers such as John *Calvin ascribed disciplinary duties within the church to elders. Not necessarily a negative term, the meaning of church discipline is essentially the same as Christian discipleship, which naturally involves a corrective aspect where disobedience is concerned (Mt 18:15-20). Where faithful admonition is rejected, church discipline leads to suspension from the *Lord's Supper and finally the excommunication of those who persistently reject *repentance.

church, visible and invisible. The visible church refers to people who profess *faith in Jesus and participate in a local church; this includes those who are feigning this faith. The invisible church refers to those who are true Christians by virtue of God's *election and *union with Christ, a group known perfectly only by God. Several Reformed *confessions indicate that the visible and invisible churches only partially correspond, explaining why the visible church will contain a mixture of believers and unbelievers until Jesus returns. In the meantime, *Reformed theology has often stressed the importance of pursuing *assurance of one's *salvation (i.e., of one's membership in the invisible church) and seeking the unity and purity of the visible church.

clergy. The ordained ministers of the church. The Reformers often took a very critical stance toward compromised Roman Catholic clergy, decrying ministerial corruption, the conflation of priestly power and the gulf separating clergy from laity. By contrast, they affirmed the *priesthood of all believers while at the same time exalting the high priestly role of Jesus. In other words, clergy do not have special access to God but are those members of the church gifted, called and ordained to teach the *Word of God, administer the *sacraments and carry out *church discipline. The Reformers also supported clerical *marriage and placed great emphasis on the pastoral responsibility of caring for the congregation.

Cocceius, Johannes (1603–1669). A Dutch Reformed theologian best known for his contribution to *covenant or federal theology. Building on the work of John *Calvin, Zacharias *Ursinus and Caspar Olevianus, Cocceius articulated not just two covenants—the covenant of works with Adam and the covenant of *grace after Adam—but three covenants, including the eternal covenant of redemption between the Father and the Son. This idea corresponded with a growing interest among seventeenth-century Reformed *scholasticism in God's eternal *decrees and presented an attempt to integrate these insights with *biblical theology and the relationship between the Old and New Testaments.

common grace. In distinction from God's special or saving *grace, this is unmerited divine mercy given generally to all humanity. John *Calvin presented a nascent form of this doctrine in connection with God's *general revelation, *providence and the *image of God in humanity. Later, several *Puritans, most notably Richard *Baxter, distinguished moral virtue available to all through common grace from true spiritual fruit. The most prominent propagator of this concept, however, was Abraham *Kuyper, who in his three-volume *De Gemeene Gratie* (1902–1904) emphasized the role of common grace in both restraining evil and enabling outward goodness, including perception of the truth, production of beauty and deeds of civic righteousness. Even when these activities are motivated by sinful pride, both Christians and non-Christians benefit from the delay of God's judgment on *sin and the expression of outward goodness. Most influential among the *neo-Calvinists, this idea has motivated cultural engagement and collaborations with non-Christians for cultural transformation.

compatibilism. The view that divine *sovereignty and human freedom are compatible and not mutually exclusive. The compatibilist perspective makes a distinction, common in *Reformed theology, between freedom to act according to a will enslaved to sin and freedom to act with a will liberated by the Holy Spirit. Although only God's *grace can make humans truly free, there is no contradiction between God's *providence and free human action, or between God's sovereign *salvation and the necessity of *good works. While some in the Reformed tradition reject compatibilism on logical or philosophical grounds, most affirm some variation while acknowledging the mysterious compatibility between divine and human action.

confession of faith. A formal statement of belief presenting an essential summary of the Christian faith and authoritative guide for the *doctrines and practices of a church or group of churches. Some of the most widely embraced confessional documents in the Reformed tradition include the *Westminster Standards and the Three Forms of Unity (*Belgic Confession, Canons of *Dort and the *Heidelberg Catechism). While these confessions were pivotal in forming Reformed *orthodoxy, other confessions, like the *Barmen Declaration and *Belhar Confession, arose as Reformed churches sought to be faithful in new and challenging contexts.

Congregationalism. A form of *ecclesiology that emphasizes the independent governing structures for the local church over the authority of denominations or synods. Some important congregationists, however, acknowledged a role for synods, including Robert Brown, who was the first major proponent of this polity. Congregationalism did not come to full prominence until the mid-seventeenth century. This church *polity is linked to *Luther's doctrine of the *priesthood of all believers, but Luther never affirmed strong autonomy for local congregations. As a movement, it arose within Elizabethan England through the influence of several *Puritans and Separatists. It also gained a following in France, but was sharply opposed by *Calvin's successor, Theodore *Beza; this French Congregationalist movement ended when its leader, Jean Morely, died in the St. Bartholomew's Day Massacre.

consubstantiation. Developed in opposition to *transubstantiation, this doctrine explains how the bread and wine coexist with the body and blood of Christ during the administration of the *Lord's Supper. Martin *Luther used the analogy of a heated iron to express how Christ is present in, with and under the elements, an understanding that persists within *Lutheranism. When put into the fire, the heat and iron are united; yet the iron remains iron. Likewise, the bread and wine become truly the body and blood of Christ while remaining bread and wine in reality and not only in appearance. Christologically, this doctrine depends on the *ubiquity of Christ.

conversion. The experience of *faith and *repentance by which Christians respond to God's gracious *election, effectual *calling and *regeneration and seek to live for him. Whereas some within *evangelicalism emphasize a singular conversion experience, *Reformed theology has traditionally highlighted conversion as both a singular event linked with *justification and an ongoing process allied with *sanctification since both faith and repentance are continual responsibilities (*conversio continuata*). This does not contradict the *perseverance of the saints but emphasizes instead that the entire life of the believer—and not just the beginning—should be characterized by faith and repentance. And while conversion is a responsibility, it is, like every aspect of *salvation, a gift of God's *grace.

Council of Trent (1545–1563). *Concilium Tridentinum,* the nineteenth council of the Roman Catholic Church, established the *Counter-Reformation by addressing such issues as the *mass, *justification and the relationship between Scripture and *tradition. The initial conciliatory tone toward reform became increasingly contentious over the twenty-five sessions. In the end the council defined the unity of Roman Catholicism over and against *Protestantism until the twenty-first council, Vatican II (1962–1965).

Counter-Reformation. Distinct from and eventually in reaction to the Protestant *Reformation, this was a movement to reform the Roman Catholic Church from within; the label was rejected by some in favor of the more positive *Catholic Reformation.* Although it is possible to trace the movement back to the aftermath of the Papal Schism in the fourteenth century, during which two popes claimed legitimacy, the main impetus of reform arose in the sixteenth century. Beginning at the Fifth

Lateran Council (1512–1517), several initiatives were launched for reforming the structure and life of the Roman Catholic Church, including the responsibilities of laity and lower *clergy. These trends culminated in the foundation of new religious orders directed toward closer observance of a common rule, including the Jesuits, who were leaders in spearheading reform and *mission. The *Council of Trent, which met at various times between 1545 and 1563, played a pivotal role during the Catholic Reformation, codifying Catholic *doctrine in distinction from *Protestantism and enacting internal reforms related to pastoral faithfulness and ecclesiastical *discipline.

Covenanters. Scottish *Presbyterians who opposed attempts by King Charles I of England and others to impose episcopal forms of *liturgy and church *polity on the Reformed Church in Scotland. After their initial protests were ignored, the Covenanters drew up a solemn agreement in 1638 known as the National Covenant in commitment to Christian liberty in Scotland, and a subsequent war between England and Scotland forced the English monarchy to yield to Covenanters' demands. After the Restoration in 1660, however, the Covenanters were violently persecuted during "the killing times" when *Episcopalianism was reinstated in Scotland. This persecution continued until James VII (James II in England), the last Catholic king to reign over the British Isles, fled England during the Revolution of 1688.

covenant theology. Also known as federal theology, this form of *biblical theology focuses on the way God relates to his creatures through covenants—binding relationships between God and humanity involving mutual promises and responsibilities. In *Reformed theology, this perspective traces back to *Zwingli's emphasis on God's covenant with Abraham, which he used in defense of infant *baptism. *Bullinger wrote the first full Protestant treatise defending a unified biblical covenant, although *Calvin similarly stressed the unity of God's covenant of *grace and continuities of *law and gospel in both Testaments. The covenant theology of Johannes *Cocceius, who built on the work of Calvin, Zacharias *Ursinus, Caspar Olevianus and others, is important because of the distinctions he developed between an eternal covenant of redemption between Father and Son and two basic *redemptive-historical covenants: the covenant of works and the covenant of grace. God established the covenant of works with Adam and Eve, promising life conditional on obedience, but after Adam and Eve's disobedience, God established the covenant of grace as a promise to bring victory over the devil (Gen 3:15). This covenant is reiterated in various forms throughout *redemptive history and culminates in the new covenant of Christ. Cocceius's perspective was widely received by Reformed theologians and found expression in the *Westminster Standards. Covenant theology continued to be a prominent theme in *Reformed theology in contrast to *dispensationalism, although significant debate emerged regarding the distinction between a covenant of works and a covenant of grace, which was rejected by Karl *Barth and John Murray but accepted by others in the tradition.

Cranmer, Thomas (1489–1556). An English Reformer most known for his work on the *Book of Common Prayer. Soon after graduating from Cambridge, Cranmer began his long career in the service to English royalty. Eventually, in 1532, Henry VIII named Cranmer Archbishop of Canterbury. During the reign of Edward VI, Cranmer completed his most important works, the Book of Common Prayer and the Book of Homilies, and invited to England significant Reformed theologians such as Martin *Bucer and Peter Martyr *Vermigli. Despite his death as a martyr under Mary Tudor in 1556, Cranmer is sometimes accused of pandering to royal authority and changing his theological convictions, as with his fluctuating views on Christ's *real presence in the *Lord's Supper.

Cromwell, Thomas (c. 1485–1540). An English minister of state under Henry VIII who worked heavily for church reform. Cromwell was largely responsible for the publication of the 1539 English Bible. After early stints in the French military and as a London cloth merchant, Cromwell served under Cardinal Wolsey and in the House of Commons. After Wolsey's death, he embraced *Protestantism and entered the service of King Henry VIII. He was involved in Henry's divorce from Catherine of Aragon, the dissolution of the monasteries and the separation of the Church of England from Rome. In 1540, after some failed political moves, Cromwell was executed by Henry VIII, without trial, on charges of heresy and treason.

D

Dabney, Robert Louis (1820–1898). A Southern Presbyterian theologian who supported *Old School theology and ardently opposed both theological and political liberalism. Dabney graduated from and later taught at Union Theological Seminary, wielding great influence on theological *education as a result of his *Lectures in Systematic Theology.* The chief of staff to Confederate General T. J. "Stonewall" Jackson during the American Civil War, he later wrote a biography of the general. He is remembered not only for his theological work but also controversially for his support of the Old South and for elements of racism found in his writings.

decrees, divine. The eternal purpose of God as expressed in his sovereign, hidden will, extending to whatever comes to pass, but particularly concerning *election and *salvation. The original Reformers commonly referred to God's eternal decrees, but more extended reflection arose within Reformed *scholasticism, with debates intensifying around the issues of *infralapsarianism, *supralapsarianism and the order of God's decrees. Despite these disagreements and the curtailment of decretal language in more recent theology, the Reformed tradition continues to affirm God's *sovereignty and mysterious *providence guiding all things, expressed in dynamic interplay with human responsibility and action.

dialectical theology. Also sometimes called neo-orthodoxy, this broad movement as expressed by diverse theologians such as Karl *Barth, Emil *Brunner, H. Richard *Niebuhr and Reinhold *Neibuhr protested the possible reduction of God to a mere analysis of humanity; some thought this problematic anthropological focus had become inherent in Protestant liberalism as initiated by Friedrich *Schleiermacher. Emphasizing the radical otherness of God, many associated with this protest distinguished between God's historical actions (the *revelation of the

*Word of God) and humanity's historical existence (the writing of Scripture). When God reveals himself, God veils himself, as with the crucifixion of Christ. Only when *faith upholds the tension of apprehending the invisible within the visible can it obtain *knowledge of God.

diets (or national councils). With informal origins in the fifteenth century, these conferences became the primary forums for political debate between the Holy Roman Emperor, his advisers and the German nobility in the sixteenth century. While leaders from northern Italy, Burgundy and the Swiss confederation were originally included, these representative assemblies became exclusive meetings of the imperial estates and the roots of a unified German nation. Influencing and influenced by the diverse interests of the German states and the hegemonic imperial court, the religious issues of the *German Reformation became an important part of the political debate with Martin *Luther's firm stand at the Diets of Augsburg (1518) and Worms (1521).

dispensationalism. A theological system dividing the history of redemption into separate periods (dispensations) in which God relates to his people in unique ways, first developed by Englishman John Nelson Darby (1800–1882) and primarily popularized in the United States through the *Scofield Reference Bible*. Dispensationalism differs from *covenant theology by identifying two separate peoples—Israel and the church—to whom God relates in distinct ways, thus introducing greater discontinuity into the biblical story than normally affirmed in the Reformed tradition. Given its wide-ranging influence, however, dispensationalism has been affirmed by some Reformed theologians, particularly in North America.

doctrine. The church's teaching about God and the drama of *salvation as revealed in Scripture, appropriately informed but not ruled by *tradition, experience and cultural context. In contrast with viewing doctrine as either prescribed propositions or described experiences, the Reformed tradition regards doctrine as belief about God, his *Word and his world arising out of and directing Christian *faith and life. These doctrines are typically organized according to themes and summarized in

*confessions, which bind together different communities and provide boundaries for faithful belief and practice.

doctrines of grace. Often associated in more recent history with the *five points of *Calvinism or *TULIP, the doctrines of grace were delineated by the Synod of *Dort in 1618–1619 to counter the statements issued by *Remonstrants who subscribed to the teachings of *Arminius. These *doctrines summarize a Reformed perspective on the roles of God and humanity in *salvation, affirming that it is the work of God from beginning to end. Although many Reformed theologians reject, at least in part, how these doctrines are communicated in the acronym TULIP, each point is meant to express in a different way the *sovereignty of God and his gracious action in salvation.

dogmatic theology. An orderly summary and exposition of the topics or *loci* of theology as confessed by the *church on the basis of *Scripture. The place of dogmatics in relation to other disciplines such as *biblical, *systematic, philosophical and historical theology has been a matter of significant debate. In the Reformed tradition, however, it is generally agreed that dogmatic theology involves a combination of what Herman *Bavinck called "divine authority and churchly confession." In other words, dogmatic theology presents truths of the Christian faith in a way that is not only carefully organized but also confessionally oriented. John *Calvin's *The Institutes of Christian Religion* and Zacharias *Ursinus's *Commentary on the *Heidelberg Catechism* represent nascent forms of dogmatic theology, and in the nineteenth century Heinrich Heppe compiled a famous compendium of sixteenth- and seventeenth-century *Reformed theology called *Reformed Dogmatics*, which provides a sample of the tradition's handling of various topics. Major examples of constructive Reformed dogmatics in the last two centuries include Herman Bavinck's *Reformed Dogmatics*, Karl *Barth's *Church Dogmatics* and G. C. *Berkouwer's *Studies in Dogmatics*.

Dooyeweerd, Herman (1894–1977). A Dutch *neo-Calvinist philosopher. Dooyeweerd graduated from the Free University of Amsterdam, where he later taught as professor of law for forty years. Abraham *Kuyper was a major influence as Dooyeweerd developed his political philosophy and foundational theory of creational aspects governing every sphere of life. Dooyeweerd's thought has far-reaching implications for a host of disciplines and has influenced *apologetics (including *presuppositionalism), *worldview thinking, and interdisciplinary *education in the Reformed tradition. One of Dooyeweerd's most specific legacies is *Philosophia Reformata*, a journal he cofounded with Dirk Vollenhoven in 1935, carrying on their passion for critical thinking in every area of life.

Dort (also Dordrecht), Synod and Canons of (1618–1619) A national synod of the Dutch Reformed Church convened in Dordrecht, Holland, to settle disputes arising over followers of Jacobus *Arminius. Together with many international delegates, the synod affirmed the use of the *Heidelberg Catechism and the *Belgic Confession and crafted five articles, the Canons of Dordrecht, distinguishing doctrines on *sin and God's *sovereignty in *salvation from the views of the *Remonstrants.

Dutch Reformation. The growth of *Protestantism in Holland, which was deeply intertwined with political as well as religious reform. Despite some initial enthusiasm for *Lutheranism among the Dutch, Catholic Emperor Charles V's heresy laws, beginning in 1521, quelled the spread of Lutheranism. *Anabaptism took root in the mid-sixteenth century, particularly among the common people in the southern provinces. Over one thousand Protestants were executed for their beliefs under Charles and his son Philip II, but support for *Calvinism gradually increased, beginning in the 1540s. Out of this Reformed church, born under persecution, leadership arose for political and religious freedom from the Spanish Empire. In 1572, a group of rebels under the command of William of Orange (William the Silent) took control in the northern provinces and established the parliamentary States-General. These provinces united officially in 1579 under the Union of Utrecht, which established the Reformed church as the official church but also allowed for limited religious toleration (private, not public, practice of other religious traditions). In the early seventeenth century, the *Arminian Remonstrant controversy upset this new balance, and for a time, the *Remonstrants were excluded from this policy of toleration. Eventually, however, they were granted freedom along with other Protestant dissidents, Catholics and Jews who were all allowed to establish public places of *worship in the Netherlands by the end of the seventeenth century. The initial Dutch Reformation should be distinguished from the Nadere Reformatie, or Dutch Second Reformation, which was largely a seventeenth- and early eighteenth-century movement concentrating on extending reform to every area of life.

E

ecclesiology. The study of the *church (Greek, *ekklēsia*) and its theological nature, *worship and members, including practical matters of church *polity, *offices and pastoral care. Because of its placement in the Apostles' and the Nicene Creed, the church is often considered under the heading of *pneumatology, and its essence is determined by the *marks of the church. With the rejection of the *papacy, the leaders of the *magisterial Reformation returned to the simplicity of the creedal definition and emphasized the centrality of Scripture, with *preaching and the *sacraments making visible the reality of the invisible church. Martin *Luther developed the idea of the *two kingdoms to differentiate earthly authority, such as civil *government, from the spiritual authority of the church based on the gospel of *justification by faith. With his doctrine of *election, John *Calvin emphasized the spiritual communion of the *saints as the essence of the church, further grounding the church in the *providence of God. For the *radical Reformation and *Anabaptists, the church is defined primarily according to activities and practices found in the book of Acts. Following Friedrich *Schleiermacher, one strain of modern ecclesiology has been oriented to religious experience. Karl *Barth emphasized the necessity of *prayer in framing theological reflection as a task of the church. Amid these different emphases, the presence and action of *Word and Spirit remain the fundamental impulse of Reformed ecclesiology, whether focusing on the sacraments, preaching, *liturgy, prayer, fellowship or the church's *mission.

ecumenism. From the Greek word meaning "the whole habitable earth" (*oikoumenē*), this term describes a movement for visible unity among Christian traditions rather than doctrinal hegemony. Organizations like the *World Communion of Reformed Churches seek to promote a unified Reformed identity in dialogue with other Christian traditions and missionary efforts. While numerous divisions have often marked the Reformed tradition, there has been a significant contemporary trend toward unification, as seen in the creation of the Church of South India (1947), the Church of North India (1970), the United Reformed Church in the UK (1972), and the Presbyterian Church, USA (1983). Yet many within the Reformed tradition remain fearful that such ecumenical efforts aimed at visible unity end up inordinately compromising theological and missional integrity.

education. The *Reformation wielded far-reaching influence on the education of *clergy and laity through such initiatives as vernacular Bible *translations, the establishment of schools and theological academies, and the creation and consistent use of *catechisms. Other factors contributing to the rise in Christian education and lay literacy include the spread of printed material and the influence of *humanist scholars such as *Erasmus. Many Reformed pastors, like Thomas *Chalmers, are known for their unstinting commitment to running schools and educating their parishes, and Reformed educational institutions are generally characterized by liberal arts education and dedication to *worldview formation.

Edwards, Jonathan (1703–1758). An American theologian who was a driving force behind the First *Great Awakening in the 1740s and whose writings display deep sympathy with *Calvinist convictions. After graduating from Yale in 1726, he became a pastor in Northampton, Massachusetts, where he remained until 1750, when he was dismissed for his strict views on the *Lord's Supper. Subsequently, he moved to Stockbridge, Massachusetts, as a missionary to the Native Americans, during which time he wrote some of his most mature works. Edwards eventually became president at the newly founded College of New Jersey (Princeton) but died soon after assuming the post. His 1741 sermon "Sinners in the Hands of an Angry God" was one of the opening shots of the First Great Awakening, and although its fame has distorted Edwards's overall theology, the sinner's enmity with God and the centrality of God's justice reflect important themes in his work. These ideas came to fuller expression in *Freedom of the Will* and *Original Sin*, in which Edwards articulated traditional Reformed teaching on the seriousness of *sin and the freeing *regeneration of the Holy Spirit. Edwards's impact has extended beyond theology to fields such as psychology and philosophy. For example, his *Treatise Concerning Religious Affections*, which explores the significance of emotions, experience and holy living as marks of "true religion," significantly influenced William James's *Varieties of Religious Experience*. In addition, Edwards continues to wield influence in philosophical circles for his particular expressions of theological determinism (in *Freedom of the Will*), idealism (especially in his earlier writings) and occasionalism (in *Original Sin*).

effectual calling. God's particular, inward call to the elect, in contrast to God's *universal calling to all humanity, which can be rejected. Effectual calling is commonly considered the second event in the *ordo salutis*, in which God the Father summons his people into *union with Christ for their *salvation as enabled by the Holy Spirit. Thus God both invites and effectually enables the elect to respond in *repentance and *faith since otherwise they would be unable to draw near to God, being dead in *sin.

election. Also known as *predestination, this *doctrine asserts that God chooses individuals and a people for *salvation. Historically, most in the Reformed tradition have explained this doctrine in light of the *sovereignty of God, his mercy and *grace, and the *total depravity of humanity, balanced with God's *universal calling to all humanity. The notion of unconditional election was clarified at the Synod of *Dort in response to the *Remonstrant or *Arminian emphasis on God's *foreknowledge as the basis of election. Reformed theologians usually emphasize both individual election and the corporate election of Israel and the church, although Karl *Barth promoted the view that since Christ is the Elect and Reprobate One, all humanity is elect in Christ.

English Reformation. The transition of the church in England from Catholicism to *Protestantism, the seeds of which were planted by John *Wyclif and his Lollard followers in the fourteenth century, although official reform was not established until the reign of Henry VIII. Henry's aspirations were primarily political: he needed separation from Rome to obtain a divorce. After he obtained supreme headship of the Church of England in 1534, however, he continued to enact religious reform, most radically in the dissolution of the monasteries (1536–1540). Nevertheless, Henry continued to favor the old order, so it was mostly through the work of his church advisers, Thomas *Cranmer and Thomas *Cromwell, that the English church began to solidify its Protestant identity. Under his successor, the boy king Edward VI working through his chief officer Edward Seymour, reform became even more distinctly Protestant. Under Edward, Thomas Cranmer published two editions of the *Book of Common Prayer* as well as the Protestant Forty-Two Articles. A brief but powerful setback to reform came during the five-year reign of the Catholic Mary I. The Marian reversals were counteracted by the succession of her Protestant sister, Elizabeth I. Under Elizabeth's authority, the *Thirty-Nine Articles (adapted from the earlier Forty-Two Articles) were approved as a distinctly Reformed *confession of faith for *Anglicanism. Elizabeth's long reign allowed the doctrines of the Reformation to settle more firmly in England. During the Elizabethan period, *Congregationalists and *Presbyterians gained greater influence in the dialogue, contributing to the rise of *Puritanism in the seventeenth century.

Episcopalianism. Also called episcopacy or episcopalism, this type of church *polity places the authority of the church in a united body of bishops. In contrast to this, *papacy sets the final authority of the church upon a single church *office bearer. While the New Testament terms bishop (*episcopos*) and elder (*presbyteros*) appear to be synonyms, episcopacy is distinguished from *Presbyterianism by the office of the bishop.

Acting as a head pastor of an area, the bishop directs the affairs of a diocese. If the diocese is a significant city or province, the head bishop may be called a metropolitan or an archbishop.

epistemology, Reformed. Developed in the twentieth century by Alvin Plantinga, Nicholas Wolterstorff and other philosophers, this theory of knowledge identifies belief in God's existence as a properly basic belief that may arise in experience but does not require a proof from more evident premises. While traditional theism seeks self-evident premises by which to affirm God's existence, this alternate strategy asserts that belief in God's existence or the truth of Scripture is warranted so long as the belief arises from faculties functioning as God intended. Belief in God or the deity of Christ is warranted (and counts as knowledge) just like the belief that other minds exist or that the past is real. While arguments for God's existence may be useful, *knowledge of God is based not on the reliability of evidence but on the proper functioning of the redeemed intellect. Although Plantinga's *Warranted Christian Belief* (2000) develops a number of themes found in the works of John *Calvin and Jonathan *Edwards, the designation of "Reformed epistemology" applies to this theory because it is articulated by philosophers who belong to the Reformed tradition, not because this view is characteristic of the historic Reformed tradition.

Erasmus, Desiderius (c. 1467–1536). Also known as Erasmus of Rotterdam, a preeminent *humanist scholar who was a driving force behind church reforms. Distancing theology from scholasticism and monasticism (see his essay *Praise of Folly*), his work avoids the rigidity of a system in favor of the free rationality of the *humanist scholar. Initially appealed to by both sides during the *Reformation, his views must be carefully set against his wider concern for social and ecclesial stability. His edition of the Greek New Testament would become a primary *textus receptus,* the basis for *Luther's and *Tyndale's revolutionary *translations. He later sided with Rome against the increasingly fragmented reform movements, polemicizing against Luther on *free will. Despite his desire for irenic resolution, both Rome and the Reformers ultimately rejected his attempt to compromise.

eschatology. From the Greek word for "last things" (*eschata*), this *doctrine deals not only with final matters such as Christ's return (*millennialism) and life after death, but also broader themes such as the nature of the kingdom of God in the life of the individual believer and the world. A shift toward focusing on these broader themes began in *biblical theology with a reconsideration of the apocalyptic element in Jesus' ministry. Several Reformed theologians have translated this biblical tension between the arrival of God's *kingdom and the delay of its consummation into the principle "now and not yet" in *systematic theology. Some notable examples include Herman *Ridderbos's emphasis on eschatology, not only in the Gospels but also in Pauline literature; Jürgen *Moltmann's attempts to unpack the spiritual and political nature of hope; and the "realism" found in the political theology of Reinhold *Niebuhr.

ethics. The study of human character and behavior. This discipline was not generally distinguished from other areas of Christian thought until the Enlightenment. The Reformers viewed *good works and *sanctification as the Spirit-enabled response to *justification by faith, with instruction for holy living based on the will of God in Scripture. In contrast to tendencies in *Luther, *Calvin held a more positive view of the *law and derived ethical guidelines from Scripture, *tradition and *general revelation within the framework of *sola scriptura. In addition to emphasizing *piety as a response to God's sovereign *salvation, the Reformed tradition also tends to situate ethics within the context of redemptive history, whether focusing on creation like *Kuyper and the *neo-Calvinists, emphasizing redemption and the command of God like *Barth, or placing ethics within the whole context of *covenant theology. Although Christian ethics has become a separate discipline in modern academics, the Reformed perspective maintains inseparable links between ethics, *doctrine, *liturgy and everyday life.

evangelicalism. From the Greek *euangelion*, meaning "good news," the word *evangelical* became associated during the *Reformation with the Protestant effort to recover the gospel of Jesus Christ in terms of *justification by faith and *sola gratia. As a particular movement within *Protestantism, however, evangelicalism arose within the context of eighteenth-century revivalism in Britain and the American colonies, developing from roots in *pietism and *Puritanism and influenced by pastors and theologians like John and Charles Wesley or the *Calvinists George *Whitefield and Jonathan *Edwards. It is common to identify some core characteristics of evangelicalism as devotion to Scripture, the centrality of Christ and his *atonement, the priority of *conversion and spiritual experience, and a commitment to activism expressed in proclamation of the gospel through *preaching and *evangelism along with demonstration of the gospel through *social action. Leaders and churches within the Reformed tradition have both converged with and diverged from evangelicalism at different points, as evident in the *New Light/*Old Light controversy during the *Great Awakening. This mixture of support and suspicion was also evident during the twentieth century with the rise of neo-evangelicalism as an alternative to *fundamentalism. Whereas some in the Reformed tradition embraced the *ecumenism, activism and *worldview orientation of this new evangelicalism, others were wary of its creedal reductionism, nondenominational spirit and anti-traditional tendencies. Today, while many in the Reformed tradition share the core characteristics of evangelicalism, some resist aligning with this movement in its contemporary form, and others insist on maintaining Reformed distinctives while affirming evangelical emphases.

evangelism. The proclamation of the gospel of Jesus Christ in word and deed. The goal of evangelism is to participate in God's work of bringing *salvation through *faith in Christ as enabled by the Holy Spirit. Traditionally, Reformed theologians see no contradiction between God's *predestination of the elect and the necessity of sharing the gospel with unbelievers through *preaching, conversation and relationships. Reformed evangelism has historically emphasized God's *sovereignty, the efficacious work of the Holy Spirit and the responsibility of God's people to invite others to hear and respond to the call of the gospel.

extra calvinisticum. This distinctive mark of Reformed *Christology defends the union yet distinction of Christ's divine and human natures in opposition to the *ubiquity of Christ popular within *Lutheranism. Associated with John *Calvin but widely evidenced in patristic writings, this interpretation of Chalcedon orthodoxy emphasizes the unity of Christ's two natures while maintaining that this union is without confusion of properties: the divine nature does not absorb the human nature, but each maintains its integrity. Consequently, the infinite nature of the divine Son is not contained or limited by the finite nature of the human Jesus, nor is the human nature absorbed into the divine with the ascension. This principle plays an important role in distinguishing a Reformed view of the *Lord's Supper, such as *memorialism or *real presence, from the Lutheran *consubstantiation, with one of the main Reformed concerns being to maintain the true and full humanity of the ascended Christ.

F

faith. True saving faith, as often explained, has three components: knowledge of the content of faith (*notitia*), assent to the truthfulness of what is claimed (*assensus*), and personal trust not simply that Christ died for sinners but that he died to save me (*fiducia*). Martin *Luther distinguished faith that results in *salvation from "works of love." He believed that if love is necessary for saving faith, then reliance on human *merit, rather than the merit of Christ's *atonement, is implied. While agreeing with Luther's emphasis on *justification by faith alone (*sola fide*), John *Calvin located the basis for faith in God's *election, with a necessary link between faith and love in *sanctification. He emphasized that *assurance of salvation comes from trusting in God's covenant promises.

Farel, William (Guillaume) (1489–1565). A fiery, iconoclastic preacher who was a major contributor to the *Swiss Reformation. His persistent and itinerant work established reform in Bern, Neuchâtel, Geneva and Lausanne, and incorporated the *Waldensians into the Reformation. Quick to recognize the abilities of others, he induced *Calvin to remain in Geneva and take on the mantle of Reformer. Close to *Zwingli in theological outlook, Farel revised *liturgy, established printers and trained preachers to carry the *Reformation to France. An evangelist more than a pedagogue, he continued to travel extensively later in life while pastor of Neuchâtel and produced an immense body of correspondence, both of which testify to his tireless efforts to spread reform.

federal theology. *See* covenant theology.

federal vision. A movement, also known as Auburn Avenue Theology, supporting controversial perspectives on *covenant theology, *ecclesiology, *sacraments and *justification. Proponents of the movement, which gained its title from a conference held in 2002, often decry the subjectivity and individualism of contemporary *evangelicalism and its influence on the Reformed tradition, addressing such problems by emphasizing the "objectivity" of the covenant relationship between God and his people. The most common critique of the movement is that such a "high" view of the church and sacraments eclipses and sometimes distorts *soteriology as recognized through traditional Reformed rubrics.

five points of Calvinism. *See* TULIP.

foreknowledge, divine. The comprehensive knowledge God has of the future as one facet of divine omniscience, or God's knowledge of all things. In the mainstream Reformed tradition, divine *election is not conditional on God's foreknowledge of who will believe since God's *decree, will or pleasure is the direct cause of election, making it unconditional. *Arminians argue that this perspective denies human *free will, although many Reformed theologians present a middle way, such as *compatibilism, between mechanistic determinism and libertarian free will independent from God's *decree.

Forsyth, P. T. (1848–1921). A British *Congregationalist minister and principal of Hackney College who revitalized the centrality of the *atonement for understanding the work of Jesus Christ and the *holiness of God. While educated in classical liberalism, he came to reject its presentation of the nature of the atonement. As a teacher of *systematic theology and *preaching, he revisited the traditional concepts of substitution and satisfaction, maintaining a pastoral tone in all his writings. Forsyth understood the cross as the reconciliation of the world to God and God to the world, and presented the sacrifice of

Christ as the defining event in the incarnation. He thus developed a kenotic *Christology, emphasizing the humility of the Son in his *obedience to the Father's will.

Foxe, John (1516–1587). An English Protestant church historian and martyrologist. Educated at Oxford, he became a fellow at Magdalen College until his exile to continental Europe during the reign of Mary Tudor. Foxe returned to England when Elizabeth came to power and released the English edition of his famous *Actes and Monuments of the Martyrs of the Christian Church*, commonly known today as *Foxe's Book of Martyrs*. His book documents the lives of martyrs from the time of John *Wyclif until around 1574, often quoting primary sources and describing the historical and religious contexts in which his subjects lived.

free will. Following *Augustinianism, the Reformed tradition maintains that God created human beings as free moral agents, fully capable of responding to God, but that the fall severely distorted the human will, resulting in a form of enslavement to *sin. Because of *original sin, the will cannot positively respond to God except by God's sovereign *grace, which does not negate human responsibility but restores natural freedom. All the leading Protestant Reformers shared a version of this Augustinian position, which *Luther famously defended in *On the Bondage of the Will* (1525) against the perceived *Pelagianism of *Erasmus. The Reformed view was developed more fully in distinction from *Arminian and Wesleyan perspectives on "libertarian" free will, the view that the will is free only if it is "able to do otherwise," that is, other than determined by God's will. Theologians such as Jonathan *Edwards (*The Freedom of the Will*, 1754) and others accentuated the compatibility (*compatibilism) of human responsibility and divine *sovereignty in conjunction with the *doctrines of grace.

French Confession (1559). This declaration of French Reformed *orthodoxy was *Calvin's expansion of an appeal to King Henri II for tolerance (1557), written at the Paris church's request for establishing doctrinal unity (1559). Also called the Gallican Confession and the Confession of La Rochelle, it summarizes biblical teaching and identifies with the Apostles', Nicene and Athanasian creeds.

fundamentalism. Commonly defined as combative conserva-
tism, fundamentalism emerged as a movement opposing modernist or liberal *Protestantism immediately following the First
World War. The name is taken from *The Fundamentals*, twelve
volumes of essays published from 1910 to 1915 and dedicated
to defending core Christian *doctrines, opposing biblical criticism, criticizing cultural movements such as socialism and Dar-
winism, and encouraging *evangelism and *mission. Whereas
fundamentalists originally battled for cultural hegemony, their
strategy began to shift after the Scopes Trial in 1925, when William Jennings Bryan successfully banned the teaching of evolu-
tion in schools but was subsequently ridiculed as intellectually
narrow and intolerant. In this increasingly tense environment,
fundamentalists began focusing more on separating from liberal denominations and forming their own organizations and
alliances, often rationalizing this strategy with a particular
form of *millennialism. Many in the Reformed tradition were
wary of aligning with fundamentalism, although some over-
lap did exist. For example, J. Gresham *Machen voiced similar
doctrinal concerns in *Christianity and Liberalism* and led efforts
to form Westminster Seminary and the Orthodox Presbyterian
Church as conservative alternatives to the liberal mainline. In
contrast with Machen's position, however, fundamentalism
has often treated rejection of particular political views and
social behaviors as normative, condemning practices that Machen saw no need to condemn (e.g., he did not support Prohibi-
tion). Along with growing numbers of neo-evangelicals, and in
contrast with common conceptions of fundamentalism, many
in the Reformed tradition have valued *ecumenism, *social action on behalf of the poor, and intellectual rigor.

G

general revelation. God's disclosure of himself to humanity
through creation, which is general both in its content and in
terms of those who receive it. This *revelation, though it may
be suppressed, is evident to everyone and reveals the existence
and power of God. Traditionally, Reformed theologians argue

that such revelation, apart from God's *special revelation, is not sufficient for a saving *knowledge of God as it does not include the unique self-disclosure of God found in Scripture and culminating in the person and work of Jesus the Christ. However, it is nevertheless often concluded, based on texts like Romans 1:18-32, that general revelation is sufficient for condemnation since humans suppress this revelation and live in rebellion to God.

Geneva Catechism (1537, 1542). A summary of doctrine written by John *Calvin, the later version becoming an official standard in Geneva for religious *education, particularly for children. The initial version was based on *Luther's pedagogy of *law and gospel, while the later revision, under the influence of Martin *Bucer, placed the Apostles' Creed before the Decalogue, the Lord's Prayer, Scripture and the *sacraments.

German Reformation. The period when *Protestantism was established as an ecclesial and political reality in German-speaking territories. It began with the publication of Martin *Luther's *Ninety-Five Theses (1517), was established with the Peace of Augsburg (1555) after the Schmalkaldic War, and was reaffirmed with the Peace of Westphalia (1648) after the Thirty Years' War. As reform took place within the political realities of the Holy Roman Empire, the imperial *diets became important forums for religious debates. Luther's firm stance at the diets of Augsburg (1518) and Worms (1521) sustained the momentum of reform that continued with his German *translation of the New Testament (1522) and the German *mass (1526). The *Peasants' War (1524–1526) marked the division of the *radical Reformation from the *magisterial. Luther and others defended the strong tie between reform and the *magistrate, and Argula von *Grumbach was one such apologist for reform to the German nobility. While the *Swiss Reformation developed at the same time, the conflict over the *Lord's Supper at the *Marburg Colloquy (1529) eroded hope for a unified *Protestantism. In 1530, the Schmalkaldic League was formed as a political unity of Protestant German states to ensure the freedom of each territory to choose its religious identity. *Lutheranism became more sharply defined at this time with the publication of Philipp *Melanchthon's *Augsburg Confession and Luther's *Schmalkaldic Articles (1537). While *Lutheranism dominated the Protestant identity of many German states, an important exception was the Reformed region around the southern length of the Rhine River on account of its proximity to Strasbourg, where Martin *Bucer and Katherina Schütz *Zell worked. John *Calvin participated in several disputations there, and Zacharias *Ursinus worked in Heidelberg toward a unified *Protestantism in Germany.

glorification. Sometimes identified as the final event in the *ordo salutis,* in which believers receive their complete and final redemption, are fully freed from all sin, and enjoy unhindered communion with God. Glorification, being dependent on *union with Christ, is considered a future reality yet to be experienced while also a secure reality grounded on the resurrection of Jesus and the promise of bodily resurrection for those in *union with Christ. This doctrine corresponds with the *perseverance of the saints and enables believers to endure suffering, knowing that trials are only temporary.

golden chain of salvation. *See ordo salutis.*

good works. A watchword of the *Reformation was *justification by faith and not by works, although these works are the necessary fruit or consequence of saving *faith. Rather than viewing works as either meritorious or worthless, therefore, the Reformed tradition often treats good works as the expected outworking of *salvation of believers who are enabled and empowered by the Holy Spirit to obey God's commands, grow in *assurance, increase in maturity and participate in God's *mission. As in every aspect of *sanctification, believers perform good works through constant reliance on God's *grace; they are not a means to secure God's love but are meant to grow out of the experience of divine love.

government, civil. Very different perspectives regarding civil government arose out of the *Reformation, ranging from the close links between church and state in the *magisterial Reformation to an emphasis on separation from civil affairs in the *radical Reformation. John *Calvin, for instance, maintained that the office of civil magistrate was one of the highest *vocational callings, while *Anabaptists claimed it was inappropriate for Christians to serve as magistrates. The Reformed tradition has usually recognized the separate spheres of government and church, to use the language of Abraham *Kuyper, while recognizing divine authority over both.

grace. The free, unmerited favor of God. The Reformers insisted that *salvation is accomplished by grace alone (*sola gratia*) and not on the basis of *good works or human *merit. The priority of grace is true not just of *predestination and *justification but the whole process of *sanctification and the life of *piety. Unlike some presentations of *irresistible grace, the majority Reformed presentation affirms that God's grace works in dynamic interplay with human freedom and responsibility. In addition, God not only gives grace particularly to his people but shows *common grace to all humanity in connection with his work of *providence.

Great Awakenings, First and Second. Two periods of revival occurring in America during the eighteenth and early nineteenth centuries. The First Great Awakening (c. 1735–1743) was led by theologians and pastors such as George *Whitefield and Jonathan *Edwards and was characterized by traditional *Reformed theology. The Second Great Awakening (c. 1795–1830) had less-defined leadership, although the theology of Yale professor Nathaniel Taylor, *New School Presbyterianism and the preaching of Charles Finney wielded great influence. Overall, pastors and theologians of the Second Great Awakening held a more *Arminian perspective on human *free will and *salvation, as evidenced by their *preaching.

Grumbach, Argula von (c. 1492–c. 1563). A German Reformer remembered for her defense of *Luther and the *Reformation to the German nobility. Born into a struggling Bavarian noble family, Grumbach was trained to be a maid to Emperor Maximillian's sister and learned to read and write German. After reading the works of Luther—with whom she regularly corresponded—and other Reformers, she used her knowledge of the German Scriptures to refute the *clergy who attacked the Reformers. Her criticism of the Roman Catholic Church led to her husband's removal from his position as prefect, after which she endured personal and public abuse.

H

Heidelberg Catechism (1563). This confessional statement, commissioned by Elector Fredrick III to soothe divisions between *Lutheranism and *Calvinism, was written by Zacharias *Ursinus and Caspar Olevianus in Heidelberg, Germany. Greatly appreciated for its pastoral warmth and insight, the catechism contains three parts ("Of Man's Misery," "Of Man's Deliverance" and "Of Thankfulness") that progress through the Apostles' Creed and Ten Commandments. The catechism remains a standard *confession in several Reformed denominations around the world, particularly those tracing their heritage to the *Dutch Reformation.

Helvetic Confession, First and Second (1536, 1562). The first was written by Heinrich *Bullinger and other Reformed theologians to address divisions between *Lutherans and *Calvinists, especially regarding the *Lord's Supper, and to unite Swiss Reformed churches under a single national standard. The second, originally written by Bullinger in 1561 as a personal confession, expanded upon the first and was later widely adopted as a confessional standard by Reformed churches throughout Europe.

Henry, Carl F. H. (1913–2003). American theologian, journalist and founding editor of *Christianity Today.* A graduate of Wheaton College (Illinois) and Northern Baptist Seminary, Henry served as professor of theology at Northern Baptist Seminary and later at Fuller Theological Seminary. Henry was a leading *evangelical scholar of his day, and his book *The Uneasy Conscience of Modern Fundamentalism* (1948) encouraged mainstream evangelicals to counter the isolationism of the *fundamentalist movement through *evangelism, philosophical reflection and active engagement with modern society. In contrast with various forms of liberal theology, Henry affirmed the central authority of Scripture in *God, Revelation, and Authority,* concluding that authentic *knowledge of God must come from God's own *revelation.

Hodge, Charles (1797–1878). Professor of theology and eventually president of Princeton Seminary who helped to establish the *Princeton theology prominent in nineteenth-century America.

Hodge founded and edited the *Princeton Review* and published the three-volume *Systematic Theology*, both of which had widespread influence. Hodge is often remembered for claiming that a new idea never came out of Princeton Seminary, highlighting his commitment to propagating traditional *Calvinism. Like other Princeton theologians of his time, he often linked personal *piety with a passion for *Reformed theology.

holiness. As a divine attribute, this quality signifies the purity and majesty of God, both in his triune essence and in his actions toward creation. The holiness of any part of creation, therefore, is entirely dependent on its unique relation to the holy God. By *grace and through *justification by faith, the church and individual believers are both declared holy through *union with Christ and grow in holiness by *grace as a gift of the Holy Spirit (see *sanctification). All who are set apart by God's *election are gathered through God's *effectual calling to accomplish his will and are referred to as *saints, meaning holy ones (see *priesthood of all believers). As holy, God's people are both *set apart from* the world and *set apart to* love God and serve others.

Hooker, Richard (c. 1554–1600). An English theologian most famous for his work *Of the Laws of Ecclesiastical Polity*, in which he defended the Elizabethan Settlement, arguing that a complete description of church *polity was not provided in Scripture, and therefore reason and *tradition rightfully played a role in its development. Theologically Reformed, Hooker diverged from contemporary *Puritan doctrine in his assertion that not all Catholics were reprobate and that they could be saved by *justification through faith even if they did not fully understand its meaning. His effort to unite the Church of England by focusing on what professing Christians had in common as opposed to their differences is often seen as the foundation of *Anglicanism.

Huguenots. Referring to French Protestants, the term, possibly a corruption of the German word *eidgenossen* (confederates), reflects the political circumstances of the *Reformation in France. Under the influence of *Calvin's teaching, disparate Protestant groups began organizing in 1555, which led to the founding of the French Reformed Church (Paris, 1559). Despite severe persecution, the Protestants gained civil legitimacy in France with the Edict of Nantes (1598). When Louis XIV revoked the edict, official persecution led to a Protestant exodus to Switzerland, Germany, England, Holland and North America. A remnant survived in France until the nineteenth century, when Protestants grew into a significant minority as a result of progressive toleration.

humanism, northern Renaissance. A literary and intellectual movement that influenced the Protestant *Reformation and its principles. The movement included such figures as Desiderius *Erasmus, who published the New Testament in Greek with its Latin *translation, an edition used extensively by the Reformers. Although humanism of the Renaissance in northern Europe was a cultural and intellectual movement rather than a Christian one, most humanists were Christians with theological concerns. Humanism's attention to philology and textual criticism was an important influence on the return to the biblical text and other sources (*ad fontes) among the Reformers. The humanist focus on human freedom also resonated with commitments of the Reformation, particularly *Luther's emphasis on the *priesthood of all believers. In addition, humanism influenced the concern for *education during the Reformation and shaped the use of literary and rhetorical strategies of theological writing and *preaching. The humanism of the northern Renaissance differed from the more recent secular humanism in that it accepted the importance of spiritual development in human flourishing and did not reject the value of the church in human society.

Hungarian Reformation. The period when *Protestantism was established as an ecclesial and political reality in the kingdom of Hungary. In the beginning of the sixteenth century, Hungary was a diverse, though predominantly Catholic, kingdom ruled by Catholic Habsburgs, but with large pockets of Orthodox and Jewish communities and some Ottoman Muslim influences. Some of the earliest exposure to Reformed *doctrine came through Swiss Reformer Heinrich *Bullinger's contact with Hungarian religious leaders, as well as Hungarian students studying abroad in places like

Wittenberg. Martin *Luther's teachings and writings spread quickly through the German-speaking royal cities of Hungary, although many ethnic Hungarians identified more with *Calvin than with Luther. As a result, both *Lutheran and *Calvinist congregations grew and coexisted alongside Orthodox, Jewish and Catholic communities in the early years of the Reformation. One unique aspect of Hungarian *Protestantism was a hybrid of *church polity, mostly following *Presbyterian organization but retaining the office of bishop. Reformed communities underwent persecution both from the Catholic Habsburgs and Ottoman Turks at different times, but by the end of the sixteenth century the Hungarian population was primarily Protestant.

Hus, Jan (Huss, John) (c. 1372–1415). Bohemian pre-Reformation advocate of church reform and eventual martyr. Hus was ordained and preached at Bethlehem chapel in Prague. Educated at Prague University, Hus was briefly appointed dean and rector, and, inspired by John *Wyclif, proposed various reforms that drew wide support. He was censured for his bold *preaching and wrote his major work on ecclesial reform while in exile. Though promised safe conduct to the Council of Constance, he was arrested and removed from the priesthood. As he was burned at the stake, he sang. Considered a martyr and national hero, he influenced the *Bohemian Brethren and the Reformers, though his work had focused more on clerical abuses and *ethics than on theological issues.

hyper-Calvinism. An extreme form of *Calvinism that, in its various historical manifestations, tends to deny *universal calling and thus denies the need for *evangelism through the free offer of the gospel. This perspective tends to grow out of a rationalist bent, focusing on God's eternal *decrees while remaining uncomfortable with the dynamic interplay between God's *sovereignty and human responsibility as represented in more traditional Calvinism. Consequently, the label is often used more broadly to refer to any excessively *monergistic perspective on *salvation and *irresistible grace that denies or strongly downplays the means God uses to accomplish his sovereign purposes, such as *preaching the gospel.

I

iconoclasm. In a concrete sense, the denunciation and even destruction of religious art. In 1521, Andreas Bodenstein von *Karlstadt was one of the first Reformers to denounce religious imagery as a symbolic mediation of spiritual reality, although *Luther tempered Karlstadt's iconoclastic enthusiasm with a more conservative position that held sway over later *Lutheranism. The Swiss Reformers, however, were more actively disruptive, and under the influence of *Zwingli, the Zurich *magistrate officially condemned images in churches. Despite the censorious attitude of some Reformers toward art in *worship, the *Reformation in other ways was a catalyst for creative art, as famously articulated by Abraham *Kuyper in his Stone Lectures (1898).

idolatry. The worship of false gods or an image of the one true God. During the *Reformation, Protestants initiated widespread *iconoclasm, decrying as idolatry the use of icons, sculptures, paintings and any physical representation of Christ, including the transformation of the eucharistic bread into Christ's body during the *mass. More generally, the Reformers emphasized the sinful human tendency to make anything an idol, whether people, objects or ideas, by valuing and worshiping it in place of God.

image of God (*imago dei*). A *doctrine exploring how God created humanity in his likeness. Although all the Reformers acknowledged that God created man and woman uniquely in his image, disagreements surfaced regarding the nature of this likeness to God and the extent to which it was lost with *original sin. Most *Lutherans, interpreting the image primarily in moral categories, argued for its complete corruption at the fall. Others, like John *Calvin, acknowledged that the fall brought deformity but not utter defacement and loss of the image. Along these lines, Abraham *Kuyper, following elements within the tradition, distinguished between the indestructible image-bearing being or qualities of every human and the direction or activity of human minds, hearts and wills that either reflects or distorts God's image; forms of this distinction remain widely accepted within the Reformed tradition.

imputation. The attribution of a verdict or quality from one party to another. In theology, one meaning of the term is the attribution of Adam's guilt to all humanity, known as *original sin. More commonly, imputation describes both the attribution of *sin to Christ as a suffering substitute and the attribution of Jesus' *righteousness to believers through *justification, which together constitute "double imputation." In Roman Catholic theology, justification is understood as the inward *infusion* of righteousness, which can increase or be lost. By contrast, *Reformed theology traditionally makes a greater distinction between justification as imputation of righteousness (a judicial act of God) and *sanctification as growth in righteousness (ongoing transformation), both resulting from *union with Christ and enabled by the Spirit.

indulgences. Guarantees sold by the church believed to shorten the temporal punishment Christians experienced in *purgatory for *sins they committed after being forgiven. According to Roman Catholic theology in the sixteenth century, this favor could be purchased, typically by transfer of property or money, because of the church's official access to the "Treasury of Merit" consisting of Christ's superabundantly meritorious sacrifice as well as the accumulated *merit of Mary and the *saints. Luther adamantly opposed this teaching (in his *Ninety-Five Theses and elsewhere) because, among other problems, it obscured the need for *repentance and reliance on divine authority.

infralapsarianism. From the Latin *infra* ("below" or "later than") and *lapsus* ("fall"), the belief that God's *decrees of *election and reprobation logically come after the decree to permit the fall, in contrast to *supralapsarianism. Accordingly, God judges humanity in light of *sin, not apart from it. The position argues that if election and reprobation logically preceded the fall (as in supralapsarianism), this would ultimately make God the author of sin, creating a conflict between God's love and *holiness; consequently, it would appear that God ordains people to punishment without cause. Historically, infralapsarianism is the majority position among Reformed theologians, though none of the Reformed *confessions takes a side on this issue.

Irish Articles of Religion (1615). A collection of 104 statements of faith written by Trinity College theology professor James Ussher and adopted by the Irish Episcopal Church. They incorporated the *Lambeth Articles and later served as a framework for the *Westminster Confession of Faith, although they were officially superseded by the *Thirty-Nine Articles in 1635.

Irish Reformation. The movement of *Protestantism into Ireland, commencing during the reign of Henry VIII in the sixteenth century. Reform spread in Ireland primarily through political maneuvers, as Henry sought to remove papal supremacy and establish himself as head over the Church of England and Ireland. At that time, the general population of Ireland adhered to Catholicism, paganism or a mixture of both, and the Tudor Reformation took hold primarily in areas controlled by England. While Irish academics and theologians such as James Ussher were instrumental in shaping the Reformation well beyond Ireland, as evident in the impact of the *Irish Articles of 1615, most people were left to respond to contradicting religious dictates to follow Catholicism or Protestantism depending on the preferences of the current English monarch, all presented in English to the disadvantage of a predominantly Gaelic-speaking society. While periods of Protestant revival occurred, as in Ulster's Six Mile Water Revival in the 1630s, persecution by Catholic and *Arminian ruling powers were common. After the Irish Rebellion of 1641, which left Ireland under the rule of mostly Catholic royalist sympathizers, *Cromwell began his brutal conquest of Ireland, implementing penal laws against any Irish who adhered to Roman Catholicism. In subsequent years, Ireland underwent further political changes as rulers vacillated between Catholicism and Protestantism, with varying levels of religious toleration. Thus while individual Irish Protestants made great theological contributions to the Reformed tradition, the Irish Reformation was mostly a series of military conquests and political dictates, which did little to expose ordinary people to a Reformed *worldview and *doctrine.

irresistible grace. A phrase associated with the *I* in *TULIP and intended to communicate the sovereign *grace of God in *regeneration arising from *election and leading toward final *perseverance. Numerous Reformed theologians have argued that *irresistible* is an unfortunate and even inaccurate description since it implies God working against human *free will. Reformed *confessions refer to grace "certainly, unfailingly, effectively" working in and through the elect (Canons of *Dort) or God drawing the elect toward himself, not coercively, but "freely," as they are "made willing by his grace" (*Westminster Confession). Consequently, if grace is irresistible, it is by virtue of its persuasive rather than coercive force.

J

justification by faith. An act of God's free *grace to sinners in which he not only pardons all their *sin but considers them covenant-keepers and declares them righteous in his sight. This act is not based on their own *merit but on the full obedience and satisfaction of Jesus Christ, imputed to them by God and received by *faith alone. In his famous "tower experience," Martin *Luther became convinced that the terrifying *righteousness *of* God that condemns sinners is also an "alien righteousness" *from* God—a gift—to be received freely by faith. Thus, in contrast to the conflation of justification and *sanctification within Roman Catholicism, the Reformed view as encapsulated in the *Heidelberg Catechism and *Westminster Confession of Faith is that justification is distinct from sanctification, which is a Spirit-enabled consequence of justification. Furthermore, the Reformed tradition has normally viewed the doctrine of justification *sola fide* as a core element of the gospel.

K

Karlstadt, Andreas Bodenstein von (1480–1541). A German theologian who was *Luther's senior colleague at Wittenberg, having arrived in 1505. In 1519, he debated with Luther against Eck about *indulgences, after which both Luther and Karlstadt were excommunicated. On Christmas Day in 1521, Karlstadt led the first Reformation *Lord's Supper, administering it without vestments, in the German vernacular, and distributing both elements to the laity. A more radical Reformer than Luther, he was a more adamant supporter of iconoclasm and faced accusations of rebellion during the *Peasants' War. After expulsion from Germany, he found refuge in Basel, where he later died from the plague in 1541.

kingdom of God. The rule or reign of God. It was common for many Reformers, following the *Augustinian tradition, to distinguish between the kingdom of God as Christ's rule over the church by his *grace and the kingdom of the world as the rule of civil *government. Later Reformed theologians, such as Abraham *Kuyper and other *neo-Calvinists, emphasized the unified kingdom of God encompassing all of creation, with the secular state and the church as different spheres under the overarching rule of Christ. Divergent views of the kingdom also relate to *eschatology, particularly whether Christ's *millennial reign has already been inaugurated or if we still anticipate the literal reign of Christ on earth.

knowledge of God. Intellectual understanding and experiential awareness of God. A common distinction exists in *Reformed theology between natural knowledge of God obtained through *general revelation and saving knowledge of God received through *special revelation. John *Calvin argued that all people know of God's existence through *sensus divinitatus,* an immediate awareness of God as Creator and Judge. For some theologians and apologists, this awareness provides the basis for *natural theology and provides a point of contact with unbelievers, but Karl *Barth insisted that knowledge of God as Creator is intrinsically connected to knowledge of God as Redeemer as revealed in Jesus. Regardless of these differences, Reformed theologians agree that all knowledge of God is a result of his gracious *accommodation, and always remains finite, analogical, provisional and skewed by sin, highlighting reliance on the Spirit and the community of faith.

Knox, John (1513–1572). A prominent leader of the *Scottish Reformation. Knox was born in Haddington, educated at St Andrews and ordained a Roman Catholic priest in 1536. Persuaded to the Protestant cause under the martyr George Wishart, he pastored an English congregation for five years before fleeing from persecution to Scotland and then Geneva, where he ministered to an English congregation while studying under *Calvin. After his return to Scotland, his fearless reform, fiery *preaching and theological perspective influenced the Scottish Parliament's rejection of the *papacy in 1560 and their adoption of the *Scots Confession coauthored by Knox.

Kuyper, Abraham (1837–1920). Dutch pastor, theologian and politician associated with the rise of *neo-Calvinism in Europe and North America. Kuyper became disillusioned with Dutch liberalism and poured his energy into promoting an alternative by establishing two newspapers, forming the Anti-Revolutionary Party, founding the Free University of Amsterdam and writing hundreds of essays and books. His most famous publication remains *Lectures on Calvinism,* originally delivered at Princeton in 1898 and articulating a Calvinist perspective on history, religion, politics, science and art, with an emphasis on *common grace. Kuyper labored toward his social ideal, even serving for a short time as prime minister, while advocating the separation of church and state.

L

Lambeth Articles (1595). Nine statements composed by Church of England Calvinists under the authority of Archbishop John Whitgift, defining their belief in *predestination and *perseverance of the saints. The articles did not receive royal approval to become authorized but were later assimilated into the *Irish Articles of Religion (1615).

Latimer, Hugh (c. 1485–1555). An English Reformer and preacher known for the emphasis on *social action and Christian *piety in his *preaching. Latimer became a priest after graduating from Cambridge. He lost favor with the Roman Catholic Church in the 1520s because of his Protestant sympathies, but won favor with King Henry VIII and was named bishop of Worcester in 1535. He was forced to resign this post when the king enacted the Six Articles, which prevented the spread of *Protestantism. He was most popular under Edward VI, but with the succession of the Catholic Mary Tudor, he was martyred in 1555.

law and gospel. This phrase describes the relationship between the Old Testament—more specifically the will of God as communicated in the Torah and Ten Commandments—and the New Testament and the good news of Jesus. Historically, *Lutheran theology favors a more distinct division between condemnatory law and justifying gospel, whereas *Reformed theology emphasizes a positive third use of the law for Christians under the gospel, whereby the law does not simply show us our sin but also helps us know how to live our lives before the holy God. Furthermore, whereas Reformed theologians make this distinction, many also recognize that the law itself is a gift, and thus God's grace precedes the law and enables both freedom from the law's curse and the ability to obey.

law, three uses. A distinction made by many Reformers, notably John *Calvin, between three different functions of the moral law as revealed in Scripture. The first or civil use of the law is its role in restraining *sin and promoting order within society as a whole, to the extent that civil laws are based on God's moral law. The second or pedagogical use is the law's power to convict sinners and drive them to Christ for mercy and forgiveness. The third or normative use of the law is its ability to provide a beautiful blueprint for holy living, and is therefore an entirely positive function.

liturgy. As the form or order of public *worship, *Protestants retained some elements from Catholic liturgy while reformulating others. For example, although Protestant liturgies contained *prayers and songs, they were much more responsive and participatory than their precedents. Protestants commonly criticized the *sacerdotalism and sacramentalism of Roman Catholic *mass and preferred a liturgy of the *Word featuring Scripture reading and *preaching. Most Reformed traditions crafted liturgical guides, such as the *Book of Common Prayer, which included orders of service for public worship as well as guides for private worship and occasional services such as *baptism, *marriage and funerals.

Lloyd-Jones, David Martyn (1899–1981). Welsh preacher, writer and medical doctor. After medical studies and several years as a successful physician, Lloyd-Jones became the pastor of a small Welsh church and later was called to London to serve, along with G. Campbell Morgan, at Westminster Chapel. After Morgan's retirement in 1943, Lloyd-Jones served as pastor until his retirement in 1968 and was known for his exegetical *preaching and his leadership of Inter-Varsity Fellowship (now UCCF) in the United Kingdom. His call for evangelical churches to leave denominations containing theologically liberal congregations caused him to part ways with John Stott and other evangelical *Anglican leaders at the Assembly of the National Association of Evangelicals in London in 1966.

Lord's Supper (Communion). The sharing and partaking of bread and wine symbolizing the congregation's *union with Christ and communion with one another by virtue of Jesus' broken body and shed blood. In typical Reformed *liturgy, this *sacrament is prefaced with *prayer and concluded with thanksgiving so that the congregation's attention is focused on its effectiveness *sola gratia* through the blessing of the Holy Spirit. Attempting to provide an ecumenical interpretation after the *Marburg Colloquy, Reformed *orthodoxy moved beyond *memorialism, *consubstantiation and *transubstantiation with John *Calvin's interpretation of the pneumatological *real presence of Christ in the communion of fellowship signified by the outward signs. Calvin's view, however, has never been universally endorsed within the Reformed tradition; instead the tradition maintains a variety of expressions on a continuum between memorialism to forms of Calvin's view, in which the ascended Christ raises up his people into heaven by the Spirit to commune with them there.

Luther, Martin (1483–1546). Influential leader of the *German Reformation. Luther was born in Eisleben to the owner of a small mining business. He enrolled at the University of Erfurt in 1501 and completed his studies four years later. Following his father's wishes, Luther planned to attend law school. But before he could begin, as the story is told, he traveled through a ferocious storm and in his fear reportedly cried out, "Help me, Saint Ann, I will become a monk." Soon after, he entered an Augustinian monastery in Erfurt. Luther's decision to join the *clergy, however, was more than just his vow to St. Ann. Luther was deeply troubled about death and being right before God, feelings that persisted throughout much of his life. In 1512, he transferred from Erfurt to Wittenberg to become professor of theology. While at Wittenberg, Luther came into conflict with the Dominican friar Johann Tetzel, who was selling *indulgences. Luther saw these as undermining both the true meaning of penance and the teaching of the gospel. In response he submitted his *Ninety-Five Theses to the Archbishop of Mainz on October 31, 1517, also posting them on the door of Wittenberg castle church. These complaints were sent to Rome but not dealt with definitively at first.

In 1518, Luther had his famous "tower experience," in which he concluded from Romans 1:17 that *justification was through faith alone, based on the gift of the *righteousness of Christ and not on one's own *good works. A year later, Luther participated in a debate with Johann van Eck, during the course of which Luther admitted that he believed the *papacy and church councils could err. In response, a papal bull was issued in 1520 calling on Luther to recant his views or be excommunicated. Luther not only refused to recant but also burned the papal bull. As a result, he was summoned to the Diet of Worms and given one more chance to recant, but Luther refused once again. As Luther was on his way back to Wittenberg, Frederick of Saxony sent men to intercept him and take him to Wartburg Castle, where he was protected from the enraged leaders of the Roman Catholic Church. While at Wartburg, Luther wrote vigorously and even began a German *translation of the Bible, which he continued to revise with his colleagues until 1534. Shortly after leaving Wartburg in 1522, Luther's reform movement faced new controversy. Other Reformers such as *Müntzer and *Karlstadt pursued more radical reform, and later the *Peasants' War in Germany was defended on the basis of Luther's teaching. Luther denounced these radical extremes, but their association with his teaching damaged his reputation.

Luther wrote one of his most famous works, *On the Bondage of the Will* (1525), in opposition to a book by *Erasmus that insisted on the unimpaired *free will of humanity in *salvation (*On the Freedom of the Will*). In the latter half of the 1520s, Luther became deeply involved with the dispute over the *Lord's Supper.

The controversy culminated in the *Marburg Colloquy (1529), which sought resolution between Luther's position of *consubstantiation and *Zwingli's position of *memorialism. In the 1530s, Luther was involved with the consolidation of *Lutheranism in the *Augsburg Confession and later *Schmalkaldic Articles in order to reach agreement with the Catholic Emperor Charles V. He died in 1546 after almost twenty years of declining health.

Lutheranism. The Christian tradition identified with the teaching of Martin *Luther and his successors, such as Philipp *Melanchthon, Martin Chemnitz and Johann Gerhard. The Roman Catholic Church excommunicated Luther and his followers after disagreements regarding key issues, especially the doctrine of *justification; they were first called Lutherans by those who viewed them as heretics. The *Book of Concord* (1580) contains the Lutheran confessional standards, although the Lutheran Church in Denmark and Norway never officially accepted confessions written after 1531. While Lutheranism holds to the *solas* of the Reformation (*sola fide, *sola gratia, *sola scriptura, *soli deo gloria, *solus Christus), it historically differs from *Calvinism in such areas as its view of the *consubstantiation of Christ's body and blood in the *Lord's Supper, the *ubiquity of Christ's humanity in opposition to *extra calvinisticum,* and the distinctive separation of *law and gospel. Despite these differences, there have been more recent efforts within Lutheranism to forge closer ties with both Catholicism and Reformed churches, including the Lutheran World Federation's joint statement with the Roman Catholic Church on the doctrine of *justification in 1999. Movements within Lutheranism, such as *pietism, have had an influence within the *Reformed tradition as well. Lutheranism remains the state church in Denmark, Sweden, Norway and Iceland and has a strong presence in Finland, Germany, the United States and Canada.

M

Machen, J. Gresham (1881–1937). A Presbyterian theologian who was a leading figure in the *fundamentalist-modernist controversy in the early twentieth century. Machen was one of the staunchest supporters of *Princeton theology at a time when American theology was becoming more modern and liberal. A professor of New Testament at Princeton, Machen left the seminary to found Westminster Theological Seminary in the hopes of preserving conservative, fundamentalist *Presbyterianism, expressed most notably in *Christianity and Liberalism* (1923). After being suspended from ministry because of his support for the Independent Board for Presbyterian Missions, he helped form the Orthodox Presbyterian Church in 1936.

magisterial Reformation. The branch of the Protestant *Reformation with closer links to civil *government (the magistrate), in contrast to the *radical Reformation. *Luther distinguished between the protection of freedom and defense against heresy (*jus reformandi*) on the one hand and the care of the church itself (*cura religionis*) on the other. As such, he barred secular authorities from control over church matters but often turned to German princes for aid in reform. *Zwingli sought a much stronger link between the church and the Zurich city council, which was later tempered when *Bullinger took the lead after Zwingli's death. *Calvin affirmed the pivotal role of civil leaders but maintained that any responsibilities required of church members must be directed toward them as citizens. In England, the monarchy was the supreme head of the church after 1534 and was the prime instigator of reform, though Parliament and church leaders such as Thomas *Cranmer also played significant roles.

Marburg Colloquy (1529). A three-day meeting between German and Swiss theologians to settle a dispute concerning the *Lord's Supper. The meeting was convened by Philip of Hesse to build a united Protestant front, hoping to provide the movement with political legitimacy. *Luther (on the German side) argued that the words of institution should be interpreted literally and that communion involves Christ's *real presence in, with and under the elements (*consubstantiation). *Zwingli (for the Swiss) argued that the words should be interpreted metaphorically as the spiritual presence of Christ. Although all signed the fifteen Marburg Articles as a sign of unity, disagreement persisted on the last article, concerning the real presence of Christ.

marks of the church. Characteristics of the true, visible *church, in distinction from the four attributes of the invisible church: one, holy, catholic and apostolic. Some Reformers, such as John *Calvin, identified two marks—pure *preaching of the Word and right administration of the *sacraments—while others, such as Zacharias *Ursinus, identified *church discipline as an additional third mark. This latter view, as outlined in the *Scots Confession and *Belgic Confession, became the majority position in the Reformed tradition, although more recent debates have considered whether there should be a fourth mark regarding a commitment to *social action and care for the poor and needy.

marriage. For Protestant Reformers, marriage was not a *sacrament imparting *grace but a gift from God rooted in creation and intended for allaying lust, raising children, experiencing love and upholding society. *Luther launched one of the first critiques of clerical celibacy, demonstrating his opinion through his marriage to Katharina von *Bora. While Luther often focused on the design of marriage to satisfy procreative drives, *Calvin articulated a more positive and covenantal view, highlighting the benefits of marital union. Though disentangling marriage from the sacramental system, the Reformed tradition still views marriage as a holy calling, with divorce and remarriage only allowable under certain circumstances, such as adultery and abandonment.

mass. Derived from the Latin dismissal from *worship, *ita missa est* (it is sent), this term refers to the Roman Catholic *liturgy as a whole. The administration of the *Lord's Supper is the central act and is traditionally interpreted using the motif of sacrifice (*sacerdotalism). The teaching of *transubstantiation is used to describe how the *real presence of Christ in the bread and wine comes through the priest's act of *prayer. By the *Reformation, much *liturgy had become a mere spectacle delivered in Latin, with actual participation increasingly limited to the *clergy.

Melanchthon, Philipp (1497–1560). A German Reformer remembered as the close friend and colleague of Martin *Luther. Melanchthon came under Luther's influence after taking a professorship in Greek at Wittenberg. In 1521, Melanchthon published *Loci Communes*, the first systematic presentation of Reformation *doctrine. Throughout the *Reformation, he strove for unity wherever possible, but at the *Marburg Colloquy, he sided with Luther against *Zwingli. While controversial because of certain aspects of doctrine that diverged from Luther's earlier theology, he remains a central figure in the development of *Lutheranism, exemplified in his role writing the *Augsburg Confession and reforming *education throughout Germany.

memorialism. The belief that the *Lord's Supper is solely an act of remembrance for Christ's sacrifice. Ulrich *Zwingli strongly rejected the notion of sacrifice in the performance of the *mass and any assumption of Christ's *real presence in or *transubstantiation of the elements of the *Lord's Supper. Instead he argued for an interpretation of the *sacraments as merely a sign of *faith present within the congregation. For this reason, he argued strongly for the congregation's participation in the Lord's Supper and for worshiping in the vernacular. His revision of the *liturgy placed great emphasis on the act of remembrance. This symbolical position of *Zwinglianism remains influential in many Reformed churches.

merit. Favor or reward from God for human *good works. This concept was at the center of the Reformation debates over *justification by faith and *sanctification. While affirming the *doctrines of grace, significant elements within the medieval church taught that, according to biblical promises, God rewards certain good works such as alms giving. Protestants rejected human merit as a means to gain God's favor on account of the pervasiveness of *sin, the nature of *faith and *prevenient grace. They objected to its use as the basis for *indulgences, in which the pope transfers *saints' unrewarded merit to another person. Merit appropriately conceived functions as an important part of Reformed *soteriology, however, particularly in the *imputation of Christ's meritorious *obedience to the believer.

millennialism. From the Latin *mille* (thousand) and also known as chiliasm, from the Greek *chilioi* (thousand), this term refers to specific *doctrines and debates regarding *eschatology and the thousand-year reign of Christ mentioned in Revelation 20, of which there are three primary viewpoints: amillennialism, premillennialism and postmillennialism. The amillennial view, which interprets the millennium as a nonliteral age between the first and second coming of Christ, is most common among proponents of *covenant theology and the Dutch Reformed tradition. Postmillennialism, a view espoused by figures such as *Hodge, *Warfield and other *Princeton theologians, holds that Christ will return after the millennium, but differs from amillennialism in affirming that his return will be preceded by increased expansion of God's *kingdom. Premillenialism, by contrast, maintains that Christ will return before his millennial reign on earth, and most who hold to this position within the Reformed tradition are historic premillennialists—who maintain a greater unity between Israel and the church—rather than *dispensational premillenialists.

mission. The task and work of the church and individual Christians to participate in God's redemptive activity and to make him known to others with the hope that all people would love and *worship God. While some Reformed groups emphasize *evangelism as the primary means of Christian mission, others make an effort to integrate *social action and evangelism, seeing mission as the holistic activity of demonstrating and proclaiming the gospel and the *kingdom of God. Within the Reformed tradition, mission may refer specifically to working among unreached people groups and crosscultural partnerships or more broadly to *vocational calling and faithfulness in everyday life.

Moltmann, Jürgen (1926–). A German theologian who converted to Christianity while a prisoner of war following World War II. His early work defines theology in terms of hope with a consequent emphasis on *eschatology and the practice of *faith. As professor of *systematic theology at Tübingen (1967–1994), he was a fervent political activist and developed an ecumenical *Reformed theology. His later work focuses on God's suffering love as Trinity in relation to the world, further developing his insights on the nature of the *kingdom of God revealed at the cross. Clear and eloquent, his controversial propositions emphasize God's solidarity with creation and the church's commitment to *social action.

monergism. In opposition to *synergism, this position derives from the Protestant principle of *sola gratia and affirms the sole agency of God throughout the entire *ordo salutis*. Because of the implications for *soteriology, proponents seek to maintain the integrity of *justification by faith and reject any form of *Pelagianism, particularly claims concerning the *merit of *good works. The primacy of God's agency was also maintained in the Reformed view of *sanctification and its strong *pneumatology, yet these were articulated so as to preserve the validity and need of human agency in response to divine *grace.

mortification. The process of "putting to death" one's sinful nature (the old self), which continually struggles because of the reality of indwelling *sin. This process takes place in the lives of believers who, while they have been set free from sin's dominion by the indwelling Holy Spirit who unites them to Christ, are called to live in light of God's *grace as they actively work out their salvation. While some groups have encouraged strict asceticism as the means to mortification, *Reformed theology normally emphasizes that mortification, if it is truly part of *sanctification, must be accomplished through the Spirit of Christ in dynamic interplay with a believer's response of *repentance; mere human effort does not result in increased freedom from sin, even if it changes outward behavior.

Müntzer, Thomas (c. 1489–1525). A leader of the *radical Reformation, remembered for his promotion of violent rebellion through his apocalyptic, *millennial teachings. As a young German theologian, *Luther recommended Müntzer to take the pastorate at Zwickau. While in Zwickau, he was heavily influenced by medieval mysticism, preaching a theology defined by a militant *eschatology emphasizing suffering. As a leader of an *Anabaptist group, he helped lead the Peasants' War, viewing both the civil and religious leaders as godless enemies to be defeated. He was captured, tried and beheaded in 1525 for his role in the rebellion.

music. A historically disputed element of Reformed *worship in both its vocal and instrumental dimensions. Like other debates during the Protestant *Reformation, the views of *Luther and *Zwingli on music represent two ends of a spectrum, with *Calvin in the middle. For Luther, music was a gift from God to be enjoyed by the whole congregation, and he devoted himself to writing vernacular hymns and reformulating the *mass. By contrast, Zwingli banned music during worship and even dismantled organs, preferring personal, silent expressions of worship. Calvin supported simple, unaccompanied psalm singing as represented by the Genevan Psalter, an influential musical resource in the Reformed tradition. Despite differences over music in worship, the Reformers were generally united in supporting music outside the church, such as devotional hymns, organ and choral concerts, and music for social settings.

N

natural theology. Theology utilizing reason, experience and observation of creation to gain *knowledge of God or proofs of his existence. For *Calvin, humans have an awareness of God (*sensus divinitatis*) and encounter some of his attributes in nature, but sinful minds inevitably distort this awareness and prevent saving knowledge. *Neo-Calvinists such as Abraham *Kuyper, however, were open to some measure of natural theology as a result of *general revelation and *common grace. In response to this openness and particularly to the position of Emil *Brunner, Karl *Barth adamantly opposed natural theology, asserting the impossibility of knowledge of God apart from his revelation in Jesus Christ.

neo-Calvinism. A tradition with roots in nineteenth-century Holland, especially in the theology of Abraham *Kuyper and Herman *Bavinck, which was later developed philosophically by Herman *Dooyeweerd and rose in influence across North America. A major emphasis of this tradition is the detailed division of the created order into various spheres or aspects governed by God-given norms. Whereas the structure of each aspect is incorruptibly good, the direction of each has been distorted by the fall, and the purpose of God's gracious redemption is to repair this brokenness. Consequently, this perspective contributes to a *worldview encompassing every area of life and ordered according to the biblical narrative of creation-fall-redemption-consummation. Commitment to Christ's *sovereignty over and redemption of every inch of the universe influenced a strong affirmation of *vocational calling and a holistic view of divine and ecclesial *mission. Believing that by his *grace God is restoring all things to their original glory, neo-Calvinists are known for their dedication to some form of cultural transformation while being careful to maintain *sphere sovereignty. This positive stance toward *Christ and culture is often evident in a willingness to engage the arts, as exhibited in the work of Francis *Schaeffer and Hans Rookmaaker. It is important to distinguish neo-Calvinism from the recent resurgence of *Reformed theology, particularly in North America, among those often called the New Calvinists or neo-Reformed.

neo-orthodoxy. *See* dialectical theology.

Nevin, John Williamson (1803–1886). American theologian, professor and cofounder with Philip *Schaff of Mercersburg theology. Upon his graduation from Princeton Theological Seminary, Nevin worked as a theology professor at Western Theological Seminary before joining the German Reformed Seminary in Mercersburg. His German Reformed convictions led him to oppose both revivalism and *Princeton theology with a unique fusion of German idealism and American *Reformed theology. The resulting Mercersburg theology was characterized by a dependence on the *Heidelberg catechism, an understanding of the *atonement as accomplished by the person of Christ instead of his work, substantial *ecumenism, criticism of revival and a central focus on the *sacraments.

New Lights. Supporters of theologians and preachers in the First *Great Awakening, such as Jonathan *Edwards and George *Whitefield, who emphasized the importance of spiritual experience and *piety in the Christian life. New Lights defended the Great Awakening against the *Old Lights, arguing that spiritual awakening was the work of God leading to true *conversion and real Christian experience, although they did not condone organized revivals, deemed spiritually and socially chaotic. The term *New Lights* is also more broadly used to refer to groups promoting or supporting change in other Christian and religious movements.

New School Presbyterians. A group within mid-nineteenth-century American *Presbyterianism that departed from traditional *Calvinist doctrines under the leadership of theologians such as Nathaniel Taylor. The revivalism promoted by New School theologians and pastors, such as Charles Finney, was more *Arminian than the Calvinist revivals of the First *Great Awakening. A schism between *Old School and New School occurred in 1837 over theological differences, the New School's desire to merge with *Congregationalists, and slavery. A further schism occurred within both groups in 1861 during the American Civil War, leaving both Old and New Schools with Southern and Northern factions. The Southern Schools reunited in 1864, and the Northern Schools reunited in 1869.

Newbigin, Lesslie (1909–1998). Church of Scotland missionary to India, associate general secretary of the World Council of Churches and eventually bishop of Madras for the Church of South India. While he wrote numerous important works, upon retirement Newbigin produced several especially influential analyses of Christianity and Western culture. He argued that modernity defined religion as a private act and inappropriately subordinated truth to the scientific method. He emphasized that bold, personal commitment is requisite for knowing the truth, outlined the public nature of Christianity and demonstrated a gospel-saturated *ethics. His ecumenical work resulted in the expansion of *missions in the World Council of Churches and The Gospel and Our Culture Programme in the British Council of Churches.

Niebuhr, H. Richard (1894–1962). An American theologian who taught at Yale Divinity School for over thirty years. Similar to many contemporaries in *Reformed theology, he was both deeply influenced by and dissatisfied with nineteenth-century theological liberalism. He wrote extensively on the historical nature of *faith in relation to contemporary social values. Like *Barth, he nevertheless emphasized the freedom of God to speak and act within history and how the Christian witness thus transforms human society. With his older brother, Reinhold *Niebuhr, he exercised enormous influence on *evangelicalism's understanding of politics and culture. His book *Christ and Culture* presents a modern attempt at rethinking political theology in the tradition of Augustine and Jonathan *Edwards.

Niebuhr, Reinhold (1892–1971). Elder brother of *H. Richard Niebuhr, a professor of practical theology at Union Theological Seminary (1928–1960) who reclaimed a political voice for *Reformed theology and influenced twentieth-century political thought with his Christian realism. During his tenure as a politically outspoken pastor of a Detroit congregation in the 1920s, and stimulated by *dialectical theology from Europe in the 1930s, he moved beyond theological liberalism in order to take into account a more robust theological account of human experience in society, particularly with regard to suffering. His call for the church's involvement in large social issues has influenced important figures such as Martin Luther King Jr. and Dietrich *Bonhoeffer.

Ninety-Five Theses (1517). Created by Martin *Luther, these theological and practical propositions challenged common beliefs and practices of the church, particularly concerning *indulgences, *repentance and forgiveness of *sin. Luther posted his theses for discussion at Wittenberg University, and being widely disseminated and discussed, they served as a catalyst for further theological and ecclesiological reform.

North American Presbyterian and Reformed Council (NAPARC). An association of conservative Presbyterian and Reformed denominations in the United States and Canada that work together on the basis of their shared commitment to the authority of Scripture and its *doctrine as articulated in the *Heidelberg Catechism, *Belgic Confession, Canons of *Dort and *Westminster Standards. The purpose of NAPARC is to facilitate cross-denominational conversation and cooperation in a number of areas, including the appointment of joint study committees, *missions, relief work and initiatives in Christian *education.

O

obedience of Christ, active and passive. Also referred to by the Latin terms, *obedientia activa* and *obedientia passiva*, active and passive obedience refers to the complete *righteousness of Christ, specifically as it relates to the doctrine of *imputation.

In contrast to humanity's disobedience, Christ exhibited perfect obedience during his time on earth. Thus Christ's perfect adherence to the moral law is referred to as his active obedience, and the death he willingly suffered (i.e., his passion) is commonly referred to as his passive obedience. In *Reformed theology, both Christ's active obedience and his passive obedience are imputed to us for our *justification. In this "great exchange," believers' sins are imputed to Christ, and Christ's righteousness is imputed to them

offices, church. Leadership positions in the church elected by local congregations. Originally, John *Calvin delineated four distinct offices: pastors, who preach and administer *sacraments; teachers, who instruct the church in matters of *doctrine; elders, who govern local congregations; and deacons, who serve the needy. Later, it became more common in the Reformed tradition to recognize a threefold office of pastor or teaching elder, ruling elder, and deacon. In order to emphasize the equality of elders, however, some prefer to emphasize the twofold office of elder and deacon while recognizing practical role distinctions between teaching and ruling elders.

Old Lights. Supporters of eighteenth-century New England theologians such as Charles Chauncy, who, influenced by an Enlightenment *worldview, taught that *faith and *doctrine should be guided by reason. Their emphasis on reason and de-emphasis on the role of *piety and spiritual experience led them to oppose the revivals of the *Great Awakening, viewing them as overly emotional experiences potentially removed from true Christianity. Although the group had Reformed roots and was composed of *Congregationalists and *Presbyterians, their theology later departed from traditional orthodoxy. The term *Old Light* is more broadly used to refer to Christian or religious groups that do not support change within an institution or movement.

Old School Presbyterians. The traditional Reformed group within American *Presbyterianism during the mid-nineteenth century, led by theologians such as Archibald *Alexander and Charles *Hodge. They identified a sharp contrast between the Calvinist revivals of the First *Great Awakening and the revivals of *New School Presbyterians such as Nathaniel Taylor and

Charles Finney, officially separating from this group in 1837. They also opposed the New School's desire to join with *Congregationalists, desiring to maintain Presbyterian *church polity. After the schism of 1837, a further schism occurred within both groups in 1861 over slavery, leaving both Old and New Schools with Southern and Northern factions. The Southern Schools reunited in 1864, and the Northern Schools reunited in 1869.

ordination. The commissioning of people called to public ministry for a lifetime of service. In contrast to the Roman Catholic view, the Reformers did not view ordination as a *sacrament establishing a hierarchy between laity and *clergy. Rather, in keeping with the *priesthood of all believers, it is an opportunity to recognize the *vocational calling and gifts of individual leaders and to charge them with responsibility to serve the church. Ordained officers in the Reformed tradition are above all seen as servants of the *Word of God, although different church *offices and responsibilities exist to serve particular needs and correspond to distinct gifts.

ordo salutis. Latin, meaning "order of salvation," and the presumed logical order by which the Holy Spirit applies the benefits of Christ's work to those in *union with him. Standard elements in this order include *election, *effectual calling, *regeneration, *faith, *repentance, *justification, adoption, *sanctification, *perseverance and *glorification. Reformed theologians beginning in the sixteenth century developed this concept based on their view of the eternal *decrees and how God then works in time, and it was advanced by Lutheran theologians in the seventeenth century in very precise ways. The basic idea of such an order, however, can be traced to biblical passages like the *golden chain in Romans 8:29-30. While debate exists over the exact order and which elements of salvation should be included in it, Reformed theologians generally agree that each element arises out of *union with Christ.

original sin. The reality of a broken relationship with God imputed to all humanity as a result of the first *sin of Adam and Eve as representatives of humanity. While debate exists within the Reformed tradition regarding the precise nature and effects of original sin, such as the extent to which it destroys the *image of God, there is general agreement that it affects every person in their entirety (e.g., reason, will, affections, body) and that the guilt of original sin can only be removed through the work of Christ received by *faith, and not simply through *baptism. While *Calvin emphasized the *imputation of original sin from Adam and Eve, *Luther highlighted the personal nature of original sin as involving not just alien guilt but an active proclivity to *sin, which continues to influence but does not control believers with wills freed to love Christ.

Orr, James (1844–1913). A Scottish *Presbyterian minister, professor of church history at United Presbyterian College, and later professor of *systematic theology and *apologetics at Trinity College in Glasgow. Orr was a leading opponent of Ritschlian liberal theology and the subjective turn in modern theology. He articulated Christianity as an objective *worldview derived from the authoritative *revelation of God in Scripture. In addition to wielding influence through international lectures and prolific publications, Orr was a prominent leader in the unification of the Free Church and United Presbyterian Church of Scotland in 1900.

orthodoxy, Reformed. *See* scholasticism, Reformed.

Osiander, Andreas (1498–1552). A German Reformer from Nuremberg. Osiander was ordained as a priest in 1520 but joined the *Reformation efforts in 1522. He attended the *Marburg Colloquy (1529) in support of *Luther and was one signer of the *Augsburg Confession (1530). He was forced out of Nuremberg by the Leipzig Interim and in 1549 took a professorship at Königsberg. For Osiander, justification and *piety were inseparable because of the infusion of Christ's divine nature in believers, and so he opposed *Melanchthon's doctrine of *justification as mere *imputation. Osiander is also remembered for revising the Vulgate, providing the first "harmony" of the Gospels and writing a preface to Copernicus's *Concerning the Heavenly Revolution of the Planets*.

Owen, John (1616–1683). An English *Puritan theologian and prolific writer. Owen was trained at Oxford and spent his life serving in a variety of different academic, political and pastoral capacities. His career included an army chaplaincy under Oliver Cromwell, the vice chancellorship of Oxford University (1652–1657), a post as dean of Christ Church, Oxford (1651–1660), and an enormously productive writing career as a systematic and exegetical theologian. In the authoritative nineteenth-century edition, Owen's works include no fewer than twenty-four diverse and densely packed volumes, covering everything from *trinitarian theology to an extended multivolume commentary on Hebrews to some of the most penetrating devotional literature ever written.

P

Packer, J(ames) I(nnell) (1926–). A prominent evangelical Anglican theologian, professor and prolific writer. Packer was born in Britain and educated at Oxford. He was ordained in the Church of England in the early 1950s, where he rose to leadership within global *evangelicalism. In 1979, he became professor of theology at Regent College in Vancouver, where he served until his retirement. He is perhaps best known for his theologically rich and yet accessible writings, especially exemplified in his book *Knowing God*. His leadership within evangelicalism is represented by his role as general editor for the English Standard Version of the Bible, and he was recognized by *Time* magazine in 2005 as one of the twenty-five most influential evangelicals. Although some in the Reformed tradition question Packer's *ecumenism, others highly praise him for such endeavors, and much of his work is widely recognized as pivotal in helping to spur on a major resurgence of *Reformed theology among evangelicals in the past forty years.

papacy. The church *polity that has the pope in Rome as head of the visible *church. This view of church polity is distinguishable from those based on the church *office of elder (*Presbyterianism) and bishop (*Episcopalianism), though it is related to the latter. The bishop of Rome is called the pontiff, meaning "bridge builder," or the pope, meaning "father," and is the preeminent bishop, who exercises supreme and infallible authority over the Roman Catholic Church. This authority derives from the assumption of Peter's primacy as the first bishop of

Rome. Viewing the sale of *indulgences as an abuse of authority, Martin *Luther ultimately rejected papal decrees and *tradition in favor of *sola scriptura* as the source of *doctrine.

Peasants' War (1524–1526). Also called the Peasants' Revolt, this
series of insurrections in German territories ended with its
brutal suppression by the nobility. Growing primarily out of
the social and economic plight of the peasantry during the decline of feudalism, the movement incorporated several themes
from the *Reformation, such as freedom of conscience and the
*priesthood of believers. Though initially sympathetic, Martin
*Luther strongly condemned the movement in May 1525, de-
claring support for the nobility's actions. Many Lutheran leaders consequently preached passive obedience to civil authority, stemming from the theology of *two kingdoms, whereas
Reformed leaders and churches tended to advocate more active
engagement with civil concerns and *social action, based on a
different understanding of *Christ and culture.

Pelagianism. The *soteriology of Pelagius, an Irish monk, which
addressed the moral laxity of the fifth-century Roman church
by emphasizing the necessity of moral perfection and obeying
God on the basis of *free will. Pelagius rejected Augustine's
teaching on *original sin, believing that *sin exists through
individual habituation rather than ontological or legal inheri-
tance. Jesus' example of *righteousness reveals how the habits
of sin may be broken. Martin *Luther, falling resolutely on the
side of *Augustinianism, interpreted any opposition to *justification by faith as an appeal to this *synergism. Further developing Luther's *monergism, the Reformed tradition rejected
Pelagianism on account of humanity's *total depravity.

penal substitution. An *atonement theory claiming that Christ's
death on the cross in the place of sinners paid the penalty for
*sin and defeated its power. Also known as vicarious atone-
ment, this theory argues that since the punishment of sin is
death, Christ died as the substitutionary sacrifice for those
who trust in him, thus paying their debt in full. Although there
are multiple atonement theories and metaphors for the saving
significance of Christ's death, many Reformed theologians
consider penal substitution the heart of biblical *soteriology.

Perkins, William (1558–1602). Often regarded as one of the fathers of *Puritanism. Perkins was recognized during his life for his pastoral ministry and scholarship. Born in Warwickshire, England, he studied at Christ's College, Cambridge, where he later became a fellow and tutor while beginning his *preaching ministry to prisoners. He was quickly appointed rector of St. Andrew's Church, where he remained the rest of his life. Perkins wrote several biblical commentaries and many influential works on preaching, *predestination and *ethics, which influenced some of the leading Puritans of the seventeenth century, including William *Ames, Thomas Goodwin and James Ussher.

perseverance of the saints. A *doctrine not only emphasizing the necessity for Christians to endure in the *faith but also highlighting God's preservation of his adopted children. *Reformed theology asserts that since God initiates, accomplishes and applies *salvation, it is impossible for the regenerate to lose their *salvation, and therefore this concept is grounded in the doctrines of *election and God's *sovereignty. Although true believers may temporarily backslide, this doctrine affirms that such instances of rebellion are not final. Rather than providing an excuse for *antinomianism, this doctrine was intended to bring comfort to struggling believers and to encourage obedience through reliance on God's *grace.

perspicuity of Scripture. A doctrine maintaining that the gospel of Jesus Christ and the *salvation obtained through him are clearly presented in Scripture. In protest against a common view at the time prior to the *Reformation that Scripture is too complicated for ordinary people to understand apart from church *tradition and the mediation of priests, *Luther and other Reformers argued for biblical perspicuity. The doctrine influenced both their passion for Bible *translation and their preference for simple *preaching in the vernacular. Affirming perspicuity does not eradicate the need for skilled biblical interpretation or imply that every part of Scripture is plain and clear. Rather, it affirms that the message of Scripture is presented with enough clarity that it can be understood, at least at a basic level, without advanced theological or exegetical training.

pietism. Broadly speaking, a movement within Christianity that stresses personal devotion, godliness and religious experience. More specifically, pietism refers to a particular movement within seventeenth-century *Lutheranism, led by Philipp Jakob Spener (1635–1705) and A. H. Francke (1663–1727), which encouraged believers to be involved in small groups and to pursue personal devotion as a means of growth and to counter impersonal intellectualism. While some in the Reformed tradition view pietism as emphasizing experience to the detriment of intellect, others understand it as a natural partner of intellectual growth since *piety is a genuine manifestation of *regeneration. While extreme forms of pietism may lead to legalism or subjectivism, the movement continues to stimulate personal and communal growth in the global Reformed community.

piety. Often described as godly practices, spiritual habits or experiential religion, piety is a central concern of many Reformed theologians, pastors and laity. A prime example is *Puritan devotional literature, which encourages dedication to *prayer, fasting, Bible reading and self-examination. Reformed piety is Bible-centered and rooted in *grace and the gift of *faith, and as such, it has much in common with other strands of *pietism within *evangelicalism. Although different Reformed subtraditions emphasize particular expressions of piety, from personal *holiness to *social action, they are united in upholding the necessity of practical godliness as the fruit of true faith.

pneumatology. The study of the Holy Spirit's person and work. The term is derived from the Greek *pneuma* (spirit). John *Calvin is sometimes called "the theologian of the Holy Spirit" based on his emphasis on the Holy Spirit's role in *union with Christ, *sanctification, the *sacraments and every aspect of the *ordo salutis.* Following Calvin, the Reformed tradition also accentuates the Spirit's inspiration and illumination of Scripture so that *Word and Spirit are always linked. In addition, Reformed pneumatology recognizes both the Spirit's ecclesial presence through *holiness-empowering and gift-giving action and the Spirit's cosmic presence through creation, *providence and gifts of *common grace.

polity, church. The structure of church government. Three main forms of polity arose out of the Reformation: *Presbyterianism, *Episcopalianism and *Congregationalism. In Presbyterian polity, which is most common in the Reformed tradition, ruling elders are elected by the congregation and teaching elders ordained by the regional presbytery—called the classis or synod in *Dutch Reformed denominations. Ruling and teaching elders are equally responsible for governing local congregations, while presbyteries and national assemblies deal with larger issues, as outlined in the denominational *Book of Common Order or Book of Church Order. Episcopalian polity, common within every branch of *Anglicanism, maintains a hierarchical structure that gives chief authority to the bishop. Congregational polity, followed by *Baptists and several other traditions, gives autonomy to each congregation to determine membership and independently maintain alliances with other churches.

prayer. The activity of bringing all our desires and thanksgiving to God with full humility and submission to his will, confident that God will hear and respond. Understood in this way, prayer is directed to God through Christ and by the Spirit, rather than through confession to priests or prayers to *saints. There is a strong emphasis in the Reformed tradition on using Scripture as a model for prayer, exemplified in the psalms and the Lord's Prayer, while also encouraging great variety in prayer as either spontaneous or structured, corporate or individual. Reformed theologians recognize a profound mystery at the heart of prayer as the instrumental means by which God works out his sovereign will and *providence.

preaching. The proclamation and explanation of the *Word of God in Scripture with relevance to particular communities and their context. The *Reformation shaped a renaissance in biblical preaching consisting in careful exegesis and practical application. Influenced to varying degrees by ancient rhetoric, the Reformers sought to articulate the message of Scripture clearly and simply, understanding preaching as a divinely ordained means of *conversion and the power of *salvation. They emphasized that pure preaching is a *mark of the true church, giving it priority in *worship. Even as personal reading of Scripture became more common and encouraged in the sixteenth and seventeenth centuries, the Reformers commonly highlighted the distinctive power and importance of the preached word in the life of God's people.

predestination. Also known as *election, a *doctrine dealing with God's *sovereignty in the *salvation of humanity. Although many Reformed theologians make a distinction between God's active will in predestining the elect and his passive passing by of the nonelect, others emphasize a parallel action often called "double predestination," in which God actively decrees both the salvation of the elect and the damnation of the nonelect. Since most Reformed theologians take a pastoral approach toward predestination and connect it with *assurance of salvation and the responsibility of obedience, neither abandoning *evangelism nor promoting *antinomianism is an inevitable or legitimate consequence of this doctrine.

Presbyterianism. A system of church *polity consisting of rule by elders, or presbyters, originally arising out of the teaching of John *Calvin. It played a prominent role in the *Scottish Reformation and the establishment of the Church of Scotland under the leadership of John *Knox. This form of church government comprises a local session of elected elders from within a congregation, along with a teaching elder, or minister, who is called by the congregation and ordained by the presbytery. The presbytery includes the teaching and ruling elders from a group of local congregations in a particular region. Above the presbytery is the General Assembly, which has final authority in matters of church ordinance and governance and generally convenes once a year, having representatives from all presbyteries in the country. Some Presbyterian denominations also organize in synods, serving below the General Assembly. Each synod includes several presbyteries. Most Presbyterian churches adhere to the *Westminster Confession or other Reformed *confessions and *catechisms such as the *Heidelberg Catechism or the *Belgic Confession. The tradition is represented globally, with large numbers found in Scotland, the United States, South Korea and elsewhere.

presuppositionalism. A school of Christian *apologetics that claims that the fundamental assumptions of Christian truth revealed in Scripture must be presupposed in order to arrive at true knowledge. Sometimes criticized as circular reasoning, advocates of this school point out that all systems of belief rely on circularity when grounding ultimate claims. Presuppositionalists therefore deny "the myth of neutrality"—the idea that Christians and non-Christians share the same objective criteria to prove the validity of their beliefs or a common starting point for examining the reasonableness of the Christian's hope in Christ. The term for this approach originated from a derogatory description of Cornelius *Van Til's apologetic method, but it has since gained currency as a result of popular usage by Van Til's successors, including John Frame and Greg Bahnsen.

prevenient grace. God's undeserved favor given prior to justification. Two traditions arose for understanding prevenient grace. In the Reformed tradition, this is an affirmation, rooted in *Augustinianism, that God's undeserved favor precedes and enables *faith and *conversion. In contrast with *Pelagianism, Augustine emphasized the priority of God's "conquering" and life-giving grace and its transforming power. Following Augustine, the Reformed tradition has understood prevenient grace in terms of God's captivating initiative through *effectual calling and *regeneration, which fully enable and engage human responsibility and result in faith and *salvation. By contrast, the Roman Catholic perspective, articulated at the *Council of Trent, sees prevenient grace as the means by which God prepares people to accept and cooperate with their *justification. Similarly, *Arminianism understands prevenient grace as a gift that, while aiding and enabling human response to God, can be resisted on the basis of human *free will. Accordingly, in Catholicism and Arminianism, everyone receives God's prevenient grace but only some respond to it, whereas normally in *Reformed theology, it is God's elect who receive this regenerative grace.

priesthood of all believers. The belief that all Christians have direct access to and communion with God as a result of Christ's *atonement, which allows all believers to approach God the Father in Jesus by the Spirit with confidence, offering praise, seeking forgiveness and doing good in his name. The Reformers emphasized this principle in opposition to the Roman

Catholic teaching and practice of priests functioning as intermediaries between God and suppliants. While upholding the unique role of ordained *clergy, the Reformed tradition views the church as a body of priests in equal relationship with God and representing God to the world.

Princeton theology. An influential Reformed and *Presbyterian tradition in the United States during the nineteenth and early twentieth centuries, this theology developed at Princeton Seminary through the teaching and writings of scholars such as Archibald *Alexander, Charles *Hodge, B. B. *Warfield and J. Gresham *Machen. Distinctives included theology as an inductive science, Scripture as the primary source for induction, *apologetics and polemics, robust *Calvinism, commitment to the *Westminster Confession, the work of Francis *Turretin, and the influence of Scottish commonsense realism—a philosophical approach asserting that certain truths necessary for life are discovered by common sense and not deduced from other truths. Princeton theologians rejected modernist theology and were particularly opposed to German biblical criticism and liberalism. While they clung to historic *Calvinism, they regularly addressed opposing theological and scientific views, as well as contemporary American political and cultural issues.

propitiation. The satisfaction of God's just wrath toward sinners, accomplished through the sacrificial death of Jesus Christ. Many Reformed theologians consider this *doctrine to be a necessary element for understanding how the *atonement, as *penal substitution, makes possible Christ's propitiation for sins by dying in the place of sinners. This view is not intended to portray God the Father as full of wrath, in contrast to the loving Son who pacifies his angry Father; rather, it is because of God's love for the world that the Father sent his Son to be the propitiation for *sin. By this means, God is both "just and the justifier," preserving his holiness and love without compromising his character.

Protestantism. A Christian tradition arising out of the Protestant *Reformation as distinct from the Roman Catholic and Orthodox traditions. The term itself originated at the Second Diet of Speyer in 1529, where Roman Catholic leaders met to address the unified front of protest against the church within German territories. In the sixteenth century, the term was used to distinguish *Lutheranism from other reform movements, but later it referred in the broadest sense to every movement and tradition that grew out of sixteenth-century "protest" against the Roman Catholic Church and its abuses (first Lutheranism and the Reformed tradition, then *Anabaptists, *Baptists, Pentecostalism, Methodism, etc.). The status of the Church of England (*Anglicanism) within Protestantism has occasionally been debated, despite Calvinist influences, since it was originally designed as a middle way between Protestantism and Catholicism. Protestantism is usually associated with such core beliefs as the unique authority of Scripture, *justification by faith alone and the *priesthood of all believers. In Europe, the influence of the Enlightenment gave rise to Liberal Protestantism, against which Karl *Barth and others later reacted. In North America, Protestantism was shaped by such diverse sources as *Puritanism and the revivalism of the *Great Awakenings. As a result of these and other disparate influences, Protestantism in America is a diverse mixture of *Calvinism and *Arminianism as well as *evangelicalism and liberalism.

providence. The exercise of God's *sovereignty to preserve, support and direct his creation. It is founded on God's general *decree and normally accomplished by means of secondary *causes. While distinct from the special decree of *predestination, God's government of creation is inseparably oriented to his redemptive action. In addition, it is closely tied to *trinitarian theology in Reformed *orthodoxy because the *Word of God is the principle and the Holy Spirit is the power by which God maintains the created order. While some in the Reformed tradition allow for *natural theology, others, such as Karl *Barth, reject any perception of God's constant care without the insight of God's *special revelation.

purgatory. In the Roman Catholic tradition, a place of purification where some of the faithful temporarily reside after death on account of unrepentant *sin, lack of *merit or some unfitness for heaven. This element of Roman Catholic *soteriology is important for the use of *indulgences, which shorten a person's time in purgatory for a fee. *Luther denied this doctrine and subsequent Protestants rejected it, since the only possible basis for its existence was found in the Apocrypha rather than the biblical *canon. Furthermore, emphasis on *justification by faith removes the necessity for any satisfaction for sin beyond the work of Christ.

Puritanism. A Protestant movement emerging in the sixteenth century after the *English Reformation had been stifled under the Catholic reign of "Bloody Mary" (1553–1558). Puritans sought to see both the Church of England and individual Christian lives more fully reformed according to biblical standards. Although Mary's successor, Queen Elizabeth I (1558–1603), was Protestant, many felt that her attempts to foster national and religious unity by blending elements of Catholic *liturgy and *tradition with Protestant *doctrine left the church only "half reformed." Frustrated by these compromises and by immoral *clergy tolerated by the English episcopacy, Puritans like Thomas *Cartwright (1535–1603) pressed not only for *Presbyterianism (different Puritans embraced different models of church *polity) but also for pastors passionate for God's *holiness and the church's *mission. After repression under Elizabeth, Puritan hopes of institutional reform were somewhat revived under James I of England. The appointment by James's son, Charles I, of William Laud (1573–1645) as bishop of London in 1628 proved disastrous, as Laud fiercely attacked nonconforming Puritans, leading many to emigrate to the Netherlands and New England. This repression came to a brief halt after the English Civil War and the execution of Charles I in 1649, by which time Puritanism had become a major force in England and had spread to the American colonies, helping to shape the New World.

Although often misunderstood and caricatured as merely moralistic and as espousing dry rationalism, historic Puritanism was characterized by an emphasis on the final authority of Scripture, an *Augustinian view of human *sin and the need for divine *grace, and—at its heart—an abiding emphasis on the importance of personal communion with the triune God. Puritans viewed themselves as physicians of the soul, seeking to hold together a spirituality of *Word and Spirit, of heart and head, of faith and action. Scholars have observed, for example, that the Puritans explored and emphasized the continuing work of the Spirit in distinctive ways that would influence many later Protestant groups, including contemporary evangelical expressions of spirituality. Noteworthy "Puritans"—we must always remember that the name itself began as a slander and is certainly not easily defined—who helped shape the various strands of the movement, even amid its differences, include Episcopalians like James Ussher (1581–1656), Independents like Thomas Goodwin (1600–1680), Scots like George Gillespie (1613–1648), New Englanders like John Cotton (1584–1652) and Thomas Hooker (1586–1647), passionate preachers such as Stephen Marshall (1594–1655), and prolific authors who remain widely read today, including John *Owen (1616–1683), Richard *Baxter (1615–1691) and John *Bunyan (1628–1688).

Q, R

radical Reformation. Also known as the Left Wing or Third Reformation, this movement beginning in the sixteenth century encompassed a broad range of Reformers who identified neither with the Roman Catholic Church nor the *magisterial Reformation of *Luther, *Zwingli and *Calvin. Members of the radical Reformation may be loosely categorized into three groups: *Anabaptists, spiritualists and evangelical rationalists. Despite many differences between and within these groups, common factors include strong eschatological fervor, a tendency toward mysticism, believer's *baptism and extreme attitudes toward the state. Some of the foremost leaders of this movement include Thomas *Müntzer, Caspar Schwenckfeld and Andreas Bodenstein von *Karlstadt.

real presence. An interpretation of the *Lord's Supper emphasizing the actual presence of Christ over against interpretations of the *sacraments that limit the reality to remembrance. Within the Reformed tradition, Christ's real presence is articulated differently than in the traditions affirming *transubstantiation and *consubstantiation. For example, John *Calvin maintained that Christ is not present in the physical elements but that the Spirit enlivens the eyes and ears of faith to perceive and experience the reality of their communion with Christ. This stands in contrast with *Luther's consubstantiation, affirming Christ's bodily presence under the elements as well as with *Zwingli's *memorialism, a view that denies any kind of presence. Calvin's position thus attempted to mediate between Luther and Zwingli toward Martin *Bucer's hope for a unified Protestant sacramentology.

Reconstructionism, Christian. *See* theonomy.

redemptive history. The series of events recorded in Scripture by which God redeems or saves his people. From William *Perkins's *A Golden Chaine* to Jonathan *Edwards's unfinished *A History of the Work of Redemption,* Reformed overviews of God's redemptive action from creation onwards have centered on Jesus' crucifixion and resurrection. The concern to structure history around these events while taking into account the organic, progressive nature of biblical *revelation arose partly as a response to the emergence of the historical-critical method and *dispensationalism. Whereas the former fragmented biblical interpretation through scientific and historical analysis, the latter radically divided God's activity into separate eras. Charting a different path, the work of Geerhardus *Vos and Herman *Ridderbos, for example, provides a foundation for *biblical and *covenant theology that incorporates modern scholarship without sacrificing the coherence of *Reformed theology. In this way, redemptive-historical approaches aim to show how the biblical *canon displays a developmental and unified perspective.

Reformation, Protestant. A movement of theological protest and political, social and ecclesiological reform in sixteenth-century Europe. Although the beginning of the Reformation is often identified with the posting of Martin *Luther's *Ninety-Five Theses in Wittenburg, reform was fermenting simultaneously in many places throughout the Holy Roman Empire. Many reform-minded individuals, such as John *Wyclif and Jan *Hus, and several movements, including Hussites, Lollards and Waldensians, preceded Luther in challenging doctrines and practices of the Roman Catholic Church. But conditions were ideal in the early sixteenth century for a more widespread reform; contributing factors included the growing corruption in the Roman Catholic Church, the influence of northern Renaissance *humanism, *Gutenburg's invention of the printing press and rapid socio-economic changes. This unified reform, often encouraged and fostered by political leaders (cf. *magisterial Reformation), includes central ecclesial figures such as Luther, *Zwingli and *Calvin. The *radical Reformation, which includes *Anabaptists, is distinguished from the mainstream Reformation by its more extreme stance toward civil *government and by its doctrinal differences with the magisterial Reformers.

As the Reformation progressed, divisions emerged not only between magisterial and radical groups but also between *Lutheranism, *Anglicanism and the Reformed tradition. While Lutheranism spread through some parts of Germany and Scandinavia and Anglicanism arose within England and parts of Ireland, the Reformed tradition took hold throughout Bohemia, Hungary, Scotland and the Low Countries (present-day Netherlands and Belgium), in some parts of Germany, and among the *Huguenots in France. Therefore, while it is accurate to speak of the emergence of *Protestantism, this movement was not a unified whole, and it is equally important to recognize the unique character of the *Dutch, *English, *German, *Hungarian, *Irish, *Scandinavian, *Scottish and *Swiss Reformations. While reform resulted in state-supported churches in some areas, in other places reform was either successfully controlled by the *Counter-Reformation, or Protestant groups flourished under the auspices of secular authority. Because the Reformation was thoroughly enmeshed in socio-political realities, however, the ongoing turbulence of the period was not settled until the Peace of Westphalia, which ended the Thirty Years' War (1618–1648) between Protestants and the Holy Roman Empire. Indeed the contemporary configuration of European nation-states arose out of this conflict, and the dominant Christian tradition in each nation reflects the results of the Reformation.

Reformed Ecumenical Council (REC). Founded as the Reformed Ecumenical Synod in 1946, this association was the second largest international fellowship of Reformed churches, uniting twelve million people in twenty-five countries. In contrast with the *World Alliance of Reformed Churches (WARC), it sought unity through strong allegiance to the classic Reformed *confessions, though it struggled with the increasingly progressive stance of many members. Unlike other ecumenical organizations, the REC did not suspend the membership of churches that supported apartheid in South Africa, and it rejected a proposed adoption of the *Belhar Confession. Furthermore, unlike the WARC, it maintained a critical stance toward the World Council of Churches. In 2010, it merged with the WARC to form the *WCRC.

Reformed theology. As a distinct theological tradition arising out of the Protestant *Reformation, Reformed theology commonly traces its roots back to the *Swiss Reformation as represented by Ulrich *Zwingli and John *Calvin. While some distinguish Reformed theology from *Arminianism using the *TULIP acronym, the way in which some of these *doctrines are articulated—especially at the popular level—can actually misrepresent the majority Reformed perspective, and focusing solely on these points neglects many other key features of the tradition. Together with other Reformational traditions such as *Lutheranism, Reformed theology is committed to the five *solas* that prioritize God's action and *grace in Christ as the source and goal of all theology and the life of *faith (*sola fide, *sola gratia, *sola scriptura, *soli deo gloria, *solus Christus). The following eight points aim to characterize the unique combination of features that comprise Reformed theology, understood broadly.

First, Reformed theology is *canonical.* Scripture is God's unique, *special revelation and therefore the standard or canon for all theological reflection. While creation and God's *general revelation also play a vital role in Reformed theology, Scripture has primacy as the means by which believers gain *knowledge of God for *salvation and life. In fact, the label *Reformed* points first and foremost to how this tradition is open to ongoing reformation and reformulation so that its beliefs and practices correspond more faithfully to the *Word of God.

Second, Reformed theology is *creational.* Highlighting the truth that the Triune God is the Creator of all things, this tradition emphasizes the goodness and beauty of creation. The material world—including our bodies and all that is "earthy"—is not intrinsically evil, but rather created gloriously good, with humans at the pinnacle of creation fashioned in the *image of God. Such a perspective is why, for example, the Reformed tradition consistently values *vocational callings, the role of *common grace, environmental stewardship, the value of productivity and other features of embodied, creaturely life.

Third, Reformed theology is *comprehensive.* In light of this robust creational emphasis, the doctrines of *sin and redemption are necessarily framed in a holistic manner. Sin disrupts and perverts the good creation by affecting the totality of the human person (mind, will, affections, body), the totality of our relationships (with God, neighbors and the rest of creation), and the totality of the universe (it too groans in expectation of redemption). Reformed theology recognizes the extensiveness and intensiveness of sin's perverting presence, and this means Christians necessarily live in the tension between enjoying God's world and yet also fighting against sin's corruptive effects, both internally and externally. Similarly, redemption is understood in a comprehensive way as the Father through the Son and by the Spirit carries out his work of new creation. Just as sin affects everything, so God extends his love into every crack and crevice of his world as his people enter into the movement of divine grace. Because of Jesus' bodily resurrection from the dead, we know that God's work of new creation is not just an inward reality (enlightening the mind, liberating the will, awakening affections) but also a physical, social and cosmic reality. Although this work of new creation is not yet complete, Christians are sustained by the hope of Jesus' return to rule over a new heaven and new earth.

Fourth, Reformed theology is *covenantal.* As the inspired *Word of God, Scripture presents a unified story of *redemptive history and God's covenantal relationship with his people and the rest of creation. Although there are different Acts in this covenantal drama (creation, fall, Israel, Jesus, church, new creation), *biblical theology in the Reformed tradition normally recognizes an organic relationship among all the Acts as they either foreshadow or follow the core of the drama, namely, the historical person and work of Christ. With Christ as the center of this covenantal reading of Scripture, one is able to discern both continuities and discontinuities between the Old and New Testaments, valuing the unity of the whole without flattening out the distinctive parts.

Fifth, Reformed theology is *Christ-centered*. Affirming a robustly trinitarian confession, Reformed theology often emphasizes the centrality of the Son: we worship none other than God the Father, Son and Holy Spirit, yet the Father is most cleared revealed through the Son, and believers are united to the Son by the fellowship of the Spirit. Christ is the great mediator between God and humanity; God reveals himself most fully in Christ; Christ alone achieves the reconciliation of sinful humanity and divine holiness. To lose this Christocentric framework risks distorting theological and pastoral reflections. So, for example, while the Reformed tradition affirms the *sovereignty of God, it is a truth that is often framed in a Christocentric manner. The Reformers were not primarily interested in abstract hypotheses and metaphysical postulation about the divine essence and what divine power could or could not accomplish. Instead they anchored discussion about divine sovereignty in the historical Jesus who lived, died and rose again. To guide discussions of the sovereignty of God one must look to the tears and blood of Jesus on the cross and then to the power of his resurrection. When dislodged from this Christocentric perspective, Reformed views of sovereignty—and other key doctrines—easily become distorted and problematic.

Sixth, Reformed theology is *concordant*. Within the *covenant theology and redemptive-historical approach already described, God is absolutely sovereign and humans are genuinely responsible. Unlike some expressions of *hyper-Calvinism, therefore, Reformed theology normally affirms the mysterious concordance between God's *sovereignty—both in salvation and *providence—and genuine human agency, understood through the lens of *original sin and the constant necessity of grace. For example, while faith is understood as a gift from God, it is not God, but the human agent as enabled by God's grace, who does the believing. This concordant dynamic also implies a distinctive relationship between *law and gospel, as God gives what he commands; God's radical grace does not nullify Christian obedience but rather empowers and sustains it. Reformed theology does not attempt to explain comprehensively the mysterious relationship between divine and human agency but rather seeks to affirm each to the degree that each is upheld in Scripture.

Seventh, Reformed theology is *confessional*. While situated within the catholic Christian *tradition, Reformed theology generally affirms the distinctive features of several *confessions and *catechisms arising out of the *Swiss, *German, *Dutch, *English and *Scottish Reformations, such as the *Heidelberg Catechism, Canons of *Dort, *Belgic Confession and *Westminster Standards. While the Reformed confessions grew out of and exhibit harmony with classic creedal orthodoxy, they also draw attention to contributions from the Reformation, such as the organic relationship between *justification and *sanctification, a rejection of *transubstantiation in favor of *memorialism or the spiritual presence of Christ in the Lord's Supper, the threefold offices of Christ as Prophet, Priest and King, the three uses of the *law, and doctrines such as *election, adoption and Scripture as the Word of God. From this confessional foundation, Reformed theology at its best is able to maintain both its catholicity and its distinctness.

Eighth and finally, Reformed theology is *contextual*. It seeks to bring God's *revelation and the lordship of Christ to bear on all areas of life in each culture and context, impacting everything from our corporate *worship to our everyday *work. In other words, Reformed theology articulates a comprehensive *worldview, arising in response to creation, canon, creeds and confessions while always oriented toward particular contexts and aiming to interpret every idea and to orient every activity toward the glory of God in Christ.

Many believe that the way Reformed theology is expressed and lived out can be compared to three legs holding up a stool: doctrine, piety and cultural engagement. While different strands of the Reformed tradition express their "lived theology" by putting more weight on different legs, normally each of these legs remains part of the supportive structure.

regeneration. The manifestation of God's *election, regeneration refers specifically to the new birth given by the Holy Spirit, bringing life to those who were spiritually dead. Regeneration is closely associated with doctrines such as *effectual calling and *union with Christ, and this new birth results in a life of *repentance, *faith and obedience. In the Reformed tradition, *baptism serves as the outward symbol and promise of internal regeneration, demonstrating the new life that has already been or will be bestowed on the believer.

regulative principle. A principle stating that Scripture prescribes or "regulates" the permissible elements of public *worship. In contrast to the "normative principle" espoused within *Lutheranism and *Anglicanism, affirming that whatever Scripture does *not* prohibit is permissible, the regulative principle requires that elements of worship must be explicitly commanded, clearly exemplified or necessarily inferred from Scripture. In applying the regulative principle, Reformed theologians and pastors make an important distinction between biblical elements and contextual circumstances in worship. While some conservative Reformed churches prohibit instruments in worship, for example, most have not interpreted the principle so strictly, seeing a broader range of biblical elements and their contextual variations.

Remonstrants. Dutch Protestant followers of *Arminius named after the "Remonstrance" presented to the States-General in 1610. They rejected the orthodox *Calvinism of the time by articulating their divergence in five articles: (1) *election was based on God's foreknowledge of *faith; (2) Christ died not only for the elect but for all; (3) the *grace of *regeneration is available to all, though it requires the Holy Spirit; (4) grace is not *irresistible; and (5) the Bible is not clear whether we can fall from grace. They were condemned by the Synod of *Dort in 1618 and forced to recant or risk imprisonment or exile. Persecution eventually dwindled, but they were not given official toleration until 1795.

repentance. The willful turning from *sin and toward Christ in true sorrow and humility. Repentance is only possible through the work of the Holy Spirit, who gives us a greater affection for God than for sin, and as such it is closely related to the Spirit's work of *regeneration and the gift of *faith. True repentance is more than remorse; it involves *mortification and results in a change of mind, heart and action. In his *Ninety-Five Theses, *Luther noted that repentance is not merely a solitary event but constitutes the entire lives of believers.

revelation. Either the act of God disclosing himself and his will or the content of what God makes known. Revelation includes both *general and *special revelation; God discloses himself to various extents in creation, human conscience, his action in history, the incarnation, Scripture and through the Spirit in *salvation. While the historic Reformed tradition holds that God reveals himself in all these areas, some Reformed theologians, most notably Karl *Barth, have focused on Jesus Christ as the revelation of God, who is never static, but dynamically and continually encountered.

Ridderbos, Herman (1909–2007). A Dutch theologian, raised in the Reformed Church of the Netherlands, who greatly influenced the shape of Reformed *biblical theology in the twentieth century. His doctoral work was conducted under F. W. Grosheide, and after serving in the pastorate for a time, in 1943 he was appointed professor of New Testament at the Theological Seminary in Kampen, Holland. While serving there for forty years, he became particularly influential in the United States through his exposition of a *redemptive-historical interpretation of Scripture with the *kingdom of God and *eschatology at its center. Among his numerous publications, several of his most lasting contributions are found in his stimulating exposition of Paul's theology, his book *The Coming of the Kingdom* and his theological commentary on John's Gospel.

righteousness. Often interpreted abstractly as justice, this biblical concept refers to God's attribute of initiating and perfecting a right relationship with his creatures, as well as a human person's attribute of fidelity to that relationship. Based on his understanding of *justification by faith, Martin *Luther shifted the discussion away from retributive justice in accordance with the law. Instead he focused on the way God fulfills his promise toward those who have *faith, highlighting in particular the gracious *imputation of Christ's righteousness to the believer. Later

Reformed *covenant theology followed this direction, adapting Luther's *law and gospel distinction as the pattern for the old and new covenants. Holding to *monergism, Reformed *orthodoxy argues that the progress of personal righteousness and the establishing of a righteous kingdom ultimately depend on the Holy Spirit's work of *sanctification, yet this is usually conceived in a way that avoids nullifying the call for human agency in response to God's justifying act and sanctifying work.

Rutherford, Samuel (1600–1661). A Scottish theologian and political theorist. Rutherford is best remembered for his *Letters*, which speak richly of intense intimacy with Christ while offering insightful pastoral counsel, and *Lex Rex*, a critique of the doctrine of the divine right of kings. After becoming a nonconformist in the 1620s, he was exiled from his parish in Anworth to Aberdeen in 1636. He joined the Scottish *Covenanters in 1638, returned to Anworth and became professor of divinity at St. Mary's College in St Andrews in 1639. Rutherford was a commissioner to the *Westminster Assembly in 1643, returning to Scotland in 1647. Before dying of illness, he refused a deathbed summons from the restored Charles II to face charges of treason.

S

sacerdotalism. Based on the Latin word for priest (*sacerdos*), this term defines the *clergy's role of mediating the *grace of God to humanity as priests who offer the sacrifice of *mass. This view arises from the Roman Catholic *doctrine that priests, by virtue of *ordination, are invested with the power to transform the *sacraments into a vehicle of God's grace. Sacerdotalism was rejected by the Reformers in favor of the finality of the *atonement, the *threefold office of Christ and the *priesthood of all believers. The term may also refer to an overemphasis on clergy in *ecclesiology.

sacraments. Visible signs of God's promise of *salvation through *union with Christ. Their number and nature were key debates during the Reformation because of the close link between salvation, the church and sacraments in medieval theology. Developing the *Augustinian emphasis on the unity of words and physical elements, the Reformers limited the number of sacraments from seven to two, *baptism and the *Lord's Supper, since these two were directly linked to specific commands of Jesus. Furthermore, the Reformers disagreed with the Roman Catholic teaching that the act of administration possessed an innate power to confer *grace. In accordance with *justification by faith, they emphasized that the effectual power of the sacraments rests entirely on God's free action.

saints. The worldwide communion of Christians, both living and dead. In the Reformed tradition, the term is applied to all who are God's people by *election and includes both the visible and the invisible *church. Protestants rejected the Roman Catholic notion of saints as those who have attained special *merit and are worthy of veneration for their intercessory role in *salvation. The witness of the faithful is a useful example, but Reformed *ecclesiology is essentially egalitarian in denying any kind of spiritual class system and affirming the *priesthood of all believers.

sanctification. An area of *soteriology describing the *holiness of the church and the individual believer as a gift of God's *grace and *election. In Reformed *orthodoxy, sanctification is rooted in *justification by faith and elaborates the work of the Holy Spirit through the *mortification of sin and the renewal of life to active fellowship with God *sola gratia. On account of the priority of justification by faith in the gospel, the Reformers rejected the Roman Catholic teaching of infused *righteousness, whereby the individual maintains a property of *holiness through *good works. Instead they taught that holiness is gained solely by the *imputation of Jesus Christ's righteousness. The church and individuals are holy by the gift of *union with Christ. *Lutheranism and *Calvinism differ, however, regarding the extent to which the life of *sola fide may be understood as a progressive work of *grace. Martin *Luther, on account of his strong rejection of any personal *merit of *righteousness apart from *grace, emphasized that sanctification was definitive with God's declaration of the sinner's justification in Jesus Christ. In other words, for Luther the justified sinner is sanctified *by definition*. While agreeing with this definitive aspect of sanctification, John *Calvin emphasized the importance of God's progressive work of conforming believers into the likeness of Christ. Consequently, the Reformed tradition has generally given a greater role to the positive use of the *law in the Christian life than Luther's dichotomy of *law and gospel. Calvin emphasized that the *perseverance of the saints involves not merely the passive reception of eternal life but the active fellowship with and service to God and neighbor. While different Reformed theologians have highlighted particular aspects of sanctification, most draw attention to both the definitive and the progressive reality of sanctification as described in Scripture.

Scandinavian Reformation. The rise of *Protestantism as an ecclesial and political reality in Scandanavian kingdoms. Reform first took hold in Denmark in the early sixteenth century, as the urbanized country received students and other travelers bringing news of the *German Reformation. King Christian III officially changed the religion in Denmark-Norway from Catholicism to *Lutheranism in 1536. The spread of the Reformation was slower in permeating the more sparsely populated Sweden and Finland, although German populations within those countries were typically the first to embrace reform. Lutheranism became the official religion of Sweden-Finland when the Church of Sweden adopted the *Augsburg Confession in 1593. The official churches of Scandinavian countries today remain Lutheran.

Schaeffer, Francis (1912–1984). American pastor, theologian and apologist best known for founding L'Abri Fellowship. A conservative *Presbyterian, Schaeffer studied at Hampden-Sydney College, Westminster Theological Seminary and Faith Theological Seminary. He served as a pastor in the Bible Presbyterian Church and later moved to Switzerland, where he and his wife, Edith, founded L'Abri, a ministry aimed at helping both skeptics and believers grapple with Christianity while providing community and hospitality. Schaeffer believed Western culture was failing because of its dismissal of biblical Christianity, and he spoke and wrote prolifically, arguing that Christianity alone has the answers to the legitimate questions of the age. In particular, his apologetics emphasized various ways that the artistic works of non-Christians manifest a *worldview that longs for meaning and fulfillment found only in Christ.

Schaff, Philip (1819–1893). Swiss-born theologian and church historian. Educated at Tübingen, Halle and Berlin, Schaff produced a considerable body of work that influenced American *evangelicalism. While teaching at Mercersburg, Andover and Union (New York) seminaries, he promoted *ecumenism by emphasizing the Catholic and European roots of the American church. With John W. *Nevin, he developed the Mercersburg theology, integrating German romantic idealism with American *Calvinism and criticizing both revivalism and the *Princeton theology. He was influential in creating the Revised Version of the Bible and founding the American Society of Church History, and several of his multivolume works have been continuously reprinted, including *The Creeds of Christendom, History of the Christian Church* and his important edited volumes of the *Nicene and Post-Nicene Fathers.*

Schlatter, Adolf (1852–1938). A German theologian who opposed classical liberalism within German *Protestantism. With Friedrich Nietzsche as one of his teachers, Schlatter's education challenged his understanding of Christianity, but this led to a deeper affirmation of orthodoxy as well as an appreciation of academic rigor. He taught and wrote widely on theological topics, but his New Testament theology and expertise in early Judaism became his most enduring contribution. A pastoral professor, he inspired a large number of students, ministers and theologians, such as Karl *Barth and Dietrich *Bonhoeffer, who followed after his insights and example regarding the reality of the Christian gospel.

Schleiermacher, Friedrich Daniel Ernst (1768–1834). An influential German pastor, teacher and theologian who contributed to the rise of liberal *Protestantism in nineteenth-century Europe. Educated in the *pietist tradition, Schleiermacher reacted against what he perceived as abstract orthodoxy and traditionalism, seeking to reform Protestantism by fusing the life of *piety with philosophy and modern knowledge. A professor of theology and philosophy and cofounder of the University of Berlin, Schleiermacher influenced the trajectory of modern theology and hermeneutics and wrote on a range of issues including psychology, aesthetics, politics and *ethics. His *systematic theology, *The Christian Faith,* developed his early notion of religion as the feeling of absolute dependence, which he explained as the consciousness of God perfected by the work of Jesus. Others in the Reformed tradition, such Adolf *Schlatter and later Karl *Barth, opposed the liberal legacy of Schleiermacher, insisting on the historicity of *revelation and that *faith is first and foremost a covenantal relationship with the triune God rather than a "feeling" of absolute dependence.

Schleitheim Confession (1527). An *Anabaptist confession, consisting of seven articles written by Michael Sattler and endorsed by Swiss Brethren in Schleitheim. The articles summarized the Anabaptist Swiss Brethren beliefs—such as the baptism of believers, separation from the sinful world and pacifism—distinguishing them from other Protestant groups.

Schmalkaldic Articles (1537). Also called the Smalcald Articles, this confession of faith was written by Martin *Luther in preparation for a council summoned by the pope and was adopted by religious and political leaders at Schmalkalden. The articles outline, among other things, stark critiques of the Roman Catholic Church and later were incorporated into the *Book of Concord.

scholasticism, Reformed. Within *Protestantism, part of a significant movement that adapted the intricate methodologies—including linguistic precision and speculative philosophy—of medieval scholars such as Peter Lombard (c. 1095–1169), William of Ockham (1280–1348) and Thomas Aquinas (1225–1274) for the purpose of developing Lutheran and *Reformed theology. Some leading Reformers such as *Luther and *Calvin warned against scholasticism when it appeared to indulge in speculation beyond the biblical texts. Yet as the *Reformation took root and the need for theological *education arose, basic scholastic methodology proved useful and was employed by many, as exemplified in the work of Calvin's successor, Theodore *Beza. Others associated with this movement, which es-

pecially flowered in the seventeenth century, include Francis
*Turretin, John *Owen and Herman Witsius. For these theologians, scholasticism indicated more a methodology than particular content (see the work of Richard A. Muller).

Scots Confession (1560). Written by John *Knox and five other Scottish Reformers, this was the first *confession of the *Scottish Reformation. The Scottish Parliament adopted the confession in 1560, and it remained the doctrinal standard for the Church of Scotland until it was replaced by the *Westminster Standards in 1647.

Scottish Reformation. The triumph of *Protestantism as an ecclesial and political reality in Scotland. In response to the spread of Martin *Luther's teaching in Scotland, the Act of the Scots (1525) banned Lutheran *doctrine; the ban was brutally reinforced by the execution of Patrick Hamilton in St Andrews (1528). Motivated by alliance with the French and longstanding conflict with the English, Scotland remained Catholic decades after *Protestantism was adopted as the state religion of England. Finally, after French and English troops pulled out of Scotland, and influenced by the powerful *preaching of John *Knox, the Scottish Parliament abolished the authority of the *papacy in 1560 and adopted the *Scots Confession, which functioned as the authorized *confession of faith until it was replaced one hundred years later by the *Westminster Standards. Despite the official break from Rome, little was settled in Scotland since political factions persisted and leaders struggled to implement a new form of rule and to promote Protestant worship. Andrew Melville, who like John Knox had spent time in Geneva with *Calvin, played a pivotal role in instituting *Presbyterianism, although *Episcopalianism dominated until the formation of the Church of Scotland in 1690. The battle to establish the Reformation in Scotland continued throughout the seventeenth century, especially under pressure of attempts by the Stuart monarchs to impose new *liturgy and other compromises with the Catholic tradition. In response, *Covenanters formed a united resistance against these impositions, which motivated their alliance with English *Presbyterians and their presence at the *Westminster Assembly. Consequently, despite its inauguration in 1560, the

Scottish Reformation was a prolonged process of theological disputes, political battles and social reorganization, finally reaching resolution over one hundred years later.

semper reformanda. Latin, meaning "always being reformed," this phrase is an abbreviated version of the phrase *ecclesia reformata, semper reformanda* ("the church reformed and always being reformed"), which first appeared in 1674 in a devotional by Jodocus van Lodenstein, an important figure in the *Dutch Second Reformation. While prominent Reformers such as *Luther and *Calvin did not use this specific phrase, it accurately reflects the emphasis on continual reform according to Scripture that fueled the *Reformation. Like van Lodenstein, Reformed theologians insist that every church in every generation must value the gift of *tradition while submitting to the reforming Spirit who continues to lead God's people to grasp the truth as made known in the normative *revelation of Scripture.

Simons, Menno (1496–1561). A leading Anabaptist theologian. Simons was born in Friesland and ordained as a Roman Catholic priest, but immediately after his *ordination he began doubting Roman Catholic teaching on *transubstantiation, and his views of *baptism and church authority underwent similar transformations over the next sixteen years. A violent uprising in Münster (1534–1535) prompted him in 1536 to promote vigorously his Anabaptist convictions, especially pacifism, in order to prevent similar catastrophes. He wrote several devotional and theological works as an itinerant minister and hunted heretics, persuading many toward pacifistic *Anabaptism, particularly in North Germany and Holland. In a letter to Martin Micron, *Calvin opposed Simons's view that Jesus was only born *in* rather than *of* Mary and defended a *Christology that takes seriously Jesus' full humanity. After Simons's death, many of his followers came to be called Mennonites.

simul iustus et peccator. A Latin phrase, meaning "simultaneously justified and sinner," used by Martin *Luther to communicate the objective reality of *justification by faith alongside the Christian's continual struggle against *sin. According to Luther, justification means that believers have received the alien *righteousness of Christ through *imputation, which de-

stroys the power of sin that leads to death but does not eradicate the presence and pollution of sin. The sinner is justified not
through an infusion of actual righteousness that eradicates sin
but by being declared righteous because Christ's righteousness
has been credited to his account. Only through a robust view
of *union with Christ is such a declaration possible without justification becoming a "legal fiction," a charge leveled against
Protestants by Roman Catholics. In the Reformed tradition,
*sanctification includes the ongoing battle against sin (*mortification) as empowered by the Holy Spirit and his gift of *grace,
recognizing that believers will remain *simul iustus et peccator*
until their future *glorification.

sin. Any thought or action that willfully or even unintentionally
breaks God's law and falls short of God's design for creation.
The Reformed tradition has historically identified pride and
unbelief as the root of sin, a manifestation of humanity's *original sin and continual rebellion against God, which affects all of
creation. *Reformed theology maintains that God removes the
power and guilt of sin through *justification, yet Christians remain *simul iustus et peccator.* While the presence of sin remains,
it is no longer in control. *Sanctification, therefore, is a process
of dying to sin, or *mortification.

social action. The efforts of Christians on behalf of society and
the common good. The *Reformation was prompted by social
concerns as well as religious and theological ones. Reacting
against the sale of *indulgences, many of *Luther's *Ninety-
Five Theses reflected a special concern for the plight of the poor
in sixteenth-century Europe. As Luther wrote in his forty-fifth
thesis, "Christians are to be taught that he who sees a needy
man and passes him by, yet gives his money for indulgences,
does not buy papal indulgence but God's wrath." In his commentary on Galatians 2:10, Luther concluded, "After the preaching of the Gospel, the office and charge of a true and faithful
pastor is, to be mindful of the poor." Similarly, in his *Institutes
of the Christian Religion*, *Calvin insisted that "all the church
possesses, either in lands or in money, is the patrimony [i.e.,
inheritance] of the poor" (4.4.6). Consequently, the congregations Calvin oversaw in Geneva had active diaconal ministries

that served the disadvantaged, including numerous French Protestant refugees. Concern with social action also shaped the ministries of Thomas *Chalmers (1780–1847), who strove to provide *education and poverty relief among rural and urban communities in Scotland; Jonathan *Edwards (1703–1758), who served as a missionary to and advocate for Native Americans; and Karl *Barth (1886–1968), who opposed the rise of the Nazi party and anti-Semitism in Germany. Divergent viewpoints concerning *Christ and culture within the Reformed tradition, such as *neo-Calvinism and the theology of *two kingdoms, result in different perspectives on the place and importance of social action. Despite these disagreements, including whether social action should be an essential *mark of the church, there is general agreement in the Reformed tradition that social action is an integral part of *sanctification.

sola fide. A hallmark of *Luther's theology, this Latin phrase meaning "faith alone" articulates that *salvation and *justification are the work of God and received by *faith alone and not achieved by *good works, although most Reformation *confessions affirm that good works always accompany saving faith.

sola gratia. Latin phrase meaning "grace alone," a watchword of *Luther and the entire *Reformation emphasizing the sheer gift of *salvation from beginning to end, and motivating believers to place full confidence and *assurance in God's promises and power to save.

sola scriptura. This Latin phrase, meaning "Scripture alone," expresses a commitment to Scripture as uniquely authoritative in *doctrine and life, with church *tradition holding derivative rather than equal authority. This commitment does not mean, however, that Scripture is the only source for belief and practice, but that Scripture is a standard for the fittingness of insights gleaned from other sources.

soli deo gloria. A Latin expression, meaning "to God alone be glory," indicating that God alone is to be honored and worshiped on the basis of his identity and gracious acts of *salvation. This phrase summarizes the other Reformation *solas* (*sola fide,* *sola gratia,* *sola scriptura* and *solus Christus*), recognizing the God-originating uniqueness of *faith, *grace, Scripture and Christ.

solus Christus. Similar to **sola fide, solus Christus* (Christ alone) indicates that *salvation is accomplished by the sacrifice and mediation of Christ alone, and therefore that Christ is the only foundation of the church. Some Reformed theologians also emphasize that Christ alone is the *revelation and *Word of God, while other Reformed theologians recognize *revelation in creation and Scripture.

soteriology. This locus of *systematic theology deals with the *doctrine of *salvation and is closely tied to *Christology, as it explicates the saving significance of the work of Christ, and to *pneumatology, as it highlights the Spirit's application of Christ's work to the elect. In *Reformed theology, the exercise of Christ's *threefold office is the outworking of God's gracious purpose and *decrees, an exercise of his *sovereignty distinguishable from *common grace. Consequently, the central themes are **sola gratia, *solus Christus* and *justification by faith, with particular doctrines sometimes associated with *TULIP establishing the **ordo salutis.* In line with the *Augustinianism of the Reformers and their critique of Roman Catholic theology as inappropriately flirting with *Pelagianism, *synergism is rejected in favor of *monergism. Humanity's state of *original sin entails a *bondage of the will excluding any possibility of *merit and the earning of God's favor. Consequently, the restoration of *righteousness occurs only through the *imputation of the merit of Jesus Christ's active and passive *obedience. While agreeing with *Lutheranism's principle that righteousness is received only through *faith, Reformed *orthodoxy articulates a more dynamic view of *sanctification, often arguing for an inseparable bond between salvation and the expected exercise of Christian freedom in doing *good works. God's *effectual calling of his people comes through the Spirit-enabled presentation of the *Word of God through *preaching and the *sacraments. This leads to a Spirit-enabled life of *piety in *union with Christ, in which believers grow in *assurance of salvation and the restoration of the *image of God through *mortification and joyful obedience.

sovereignty of God. God's authority and power to accomplish his will as the supreme Ruler of all things. God expresses his sovereignty through his *decrees and actions, which are planned in complete independence from anything outside himself and enacted throughout *redemptive history. The Reformed tradition recognizes God's sovereignty over all creation and particularly in his acts of *predestination, *effectual calling, *justification and *glorification of his people. This sovereignty is linked paradoxically and inseparably with human responsibility in a way that resists merely mechanical determinism, although Reformed theologians differ on the nature of human *free will. God's sovereignty serves as a source of great comfort to Christians, whose hope rests in a God who controls all things for the good of his people and creation.

special revelation. The self-disclosure of the triune God manifested through his particular words and actions in history communicated in Scripture and by the Holy Spirit, preeminently through the person and work of Jesus the Son. Going beyond the basic *knowledge of God gleaned from *general revelation, special revelation provides knowledge of God and his works that is sufficient for *salvation. Therefore, special revelation always points to the saving work of Christ as communicated by *Word and Spirit.

sphere sovereignty. A feature of *neo-Calvinism originally articulated by Abraham *Kuyper, which views every area of society—family, *government, economics, church, etc.—as distinct realms of influence and authority, with each arising out of the created order and governed by the *sovereignty of God. These spheres have their legitimacy directly from God, which means, for example, that the church does not receive its legitimacy from the state and the state does not receive its legitimacy from the church. Herman *Dooyeweerd extended this idea by identifying norms in each sphere that guide appropriate understanding and activity in that area of life. This concept had a wide-ranging influence on twentieth-century Christian *education, *worldview development, *vocational calling and discussions regarding *Christ and culture, especially in the Dutch Reformed tradition.

spirituality of the church. A theological concept often attributed to Southern *Presbyterianism, emphasizing a sharp distinction between the *mission of the church and public life. According to this *doctrine, the church must not engage political or socio-economic issues and the state must not intrude into or usurp the authority of the church in "spiritual" matters. This perspective rose to prominence in America during the Civil War era through the influence of James Henry Thornwell and was later employed by some Southern Presbyterians to dissuade Reformed churches from actively promoting racial desegregation. Like those who hold the theology of *two kingdoms, exponents of this doctrine seek to avoid civil religion and the politicization of the faith. The danger in this doctrine, however, is that it can cultivate indifference toward (if not expressed support for) social injustices, as seen in the painful history of the church's struggle with racism and economic wrongs.

Spurgeon, Charles Haddon (1834–1892). English *Baptist preacher, pastor and author. While he never attended seminary and refused to be formally ordained, Spurgeon is still remembered today as the Prince of Preachers. He began *preaching as a teenager and was called to his first church in Waterbeach before the age of twenty. He was then called to pastor New Park Street Baptist Church in London, which later became the Metropolitan Tabernacle when the New Park church was outgrown. A staunch *Calvinist and supporter of *Puritan theology, Spurgeon was decidedly evangelistic in his preaching. He is also remembered for founding a pastor's college, as well as publishing numerous books and commentaries.

supralapsarianism. The *doctrine (from Latin, *supra*, "above" or "before than," and *lapsus*, "fall") that God shows his glory through dispensing his *grace and justice in time by ordaining some persons to be recipients of grace and passing over others. In distinction from *infralapsarianism, *election and reprobation are not occasioned by the fall, but are—in the mind of God—*logically* prior to the fall. Supralapsarianism rests on the premise that God's *decree has priority, and the means to carry out that decree logically follow.

Swiss Reformation. The growth of Protestantism as an ecclesial and political reality within the Swiss confederation. Church reform began in Zurich and ended with the peaceful confessional division of the confederacy into Reformed and Roman Catholic alliances. In 1525, Ulrich *Zwingli convinced Zurich to reform, and his influence spread quickly to other cantons. At the *Marburg Colloquy, Zwingli forged a strong friendship with Johannes Oecolampadius, who had been working toward the reform of Basel. In 1529, the Reformed Swiss cantons formed a federation with Martin *Bucer's Strasbourg and, after the first war of Kappel, signed a peace treaty with the Roman Catholic cantons. A dispute over the terms of the treaty, however, led to the Battle of Kappel (1531), at which Zwingli was killed. It was a decisive victory for the Roman Catholics and halted the spread of *Zwinglianism within the old confederacy. Heinrich *Bullinger succeeded Zwingli as the leader in Zurich. Other significant leaders of the Swiss Reformation included William *Farel and John *Calvin, who led reform in Geneva but whose influence extended throughout the Swiss cantons, sometimes coming into doctrinal conflict with the followers of Zwingli. Both *Zwinglianism and *Calvinism, therefore, have distinct ties to the Swiss Reformation, although these movements were shaped and continued to be influenced by ideas and actions of reform throughout Europe.

synergism. Any *soteriology that employs an independent human *free will to "work together" with God's activity of *grace in *regeneration. Early Protestants often identified such a view with *Pelagianism, rejecting it on account of the *sola gratia and in favor of *monergism. Accordingly, the Reformed tradition disputed the rise of *Arminianism by emphasizing the necessity of *grace and the inability of a human will to respond appropriately to *revelation. However, a cooperative will that is renewed by the Holy Spirit is central to the Reformed view of *justification by faith and *sanctification.

systematic theology. Theological reflection that investigates and aims to explain *doctrines in a comprehensive, coherent, ordered and reasonable manner. Different titles abound in the genre, and the term *systematic* was not used until the seventeenth century. While broadly following the order of *dogmatic theology—doctrine of God, *Christology, *soteriology, *pneumatology, *ecclesiology and *eschatology—the structure of the presentation is often modified in relation to *biblical, *covenant, *trinitarian and historical theology. The finest exemplars, however, share a concern for completeness, analytical rigor and pedagogy as compendiums of Christian truth. While preceded by the work of William *Farel and Ulrich *Zwingli, the authoritative model of a Reformed systematics is John *Calvin's *Institutes of the Christian Religion*, which in its definitive edition follows the structure of the Apostles' Creed in utilizing a trinitarian pattern. In England, some standard works were William *Perkins's *A Golden Chaine* (1590) and William *Ames's *The Marrow of Theology* (1627), though the *Westminster Standards (1646) became the abiding summary of Anglo-American Reformed theology. Significant manuals of Continental Reformed *scholasticism, both in Europe and abroad, were Johannes *Cocceius's *Summa Theologiae* (1662) and Francis *Turretin's *Institutes of Elenctic Theology* (1679). Modern theology arose with the publication of Friedrich *Schleiermacher's *The Christian Faith* (1821–1822), which viewed systematic theology as an expression of religious experiences. Some of the most significant Reformed systematic theologies in the nineteenth and twentieth centuries, which are also critical of Schleiermacher's approach, include Charles *Hodge's *Systematic Theology* (1871–1873), Herman *Bavinck's *Reformed Dogmatics* (1895–1899) and Louis *Berkhof's *Systematic Theology* (1932).

T

theologia crucis. Originally articulated by Martin *Luther, *theologia crucis* (Latin meaning "theology of the cross") is an approach to theology relying on God's *accommodation and *revelation, particularly in Jesus' suffering on the cross to provide true *knowledge and *righteousness. This approach stands in contrast to **theologia gloriae*, or the attempt to know God through speculative reason and human effort. Consequently, a theology of the cross affirms that salvation is **sola fide*, **sola gratia* and **solus Christus*, and calls believers into a life of service, self-examination and suffering **soli deo gloria*. Most Reformed theologians embrace these emphases, and the German theologian Jürgen *Moltmann is a prominent example of a theologian developing these particular themes.

theologia gloriae. In contrast to *theologia crucis, theologia gloriae* (Latin meaning "theology of glory"), which seeks *knowledge of God through speculative reason and pursues *righteousness through human effort, was opposed by Martin *Luther. A theology of glory, therefore, is not consistent with *Reformed theology because this theology denies the comprehensive effects of *sin and places inordinate confidence in human ability apart from the *grace of God in Christ alone. For some Reformed theologians like Karl *Barth, *natural theology is linked with *theologia gloriae,* while others assert that God can be known truly through both *special revelation and *general revelation.

theological aesthetics. A theological account of beauty and the arts. Although the Reformation is most widely known for its *iconoclasm, it also gave rise to a distinct approach to theological aesthetics. In general, a Reformed aesthetic privileges sound over sight, the Word over images, internal over external sensations, and action over contemplation. Other elements include a concern to portray the reality of *sin together with the miracle of *grace, to dignify everyday life and *vocational callings, and to present these truths in a simple manner. Two influential contributors to Reformed theological aesthetics are Jonathan *Edwards, who grounded beauty in the identity and action of God, and Abraham *Kuyper, who identified art as a distinct *sphere of God's good creation and argued that *Calvinism contains a distinct aesthetic.

theonomy. Literally meaning "God's law," but used to designate a variety of different ideas. For example, Paul Tillich, a German-American existentialist and theologian, used this term to describe the union of autonomous human reason with God, whom he described as "the ground of being." In the Reformed tradition, however, the term typically refers to the conviction that any Old Testament law not explicitly repealed or fulfilled in the New Testament remains binding and should be enforced in the church and civil society. This Reformed version of theonomy is also known as Christian Reconstructionism. Exponents of this view, such as Rousas John Rushdoony and Greg

Bahnsen, believe that all legislation should be rooted in divine *revelation and based on biblical principles, but not imposed by force.

Thirty-Nine Articles (1571). A set of doctrinal formulae that defined the Church of England's political and theological positions in relation to Rome and the continental *Reformation. Moderate and seeking a "middle way," it is based on *Cranmer's Forty-Two Articles (1553) and is less ambitious than other *confessions. Subscription within the Church of England is no longer obligatory, but the articles are still considered agreeable to Scripture.

threefold office of Christ. A phrase (Latin, *munus triplex*) referring to the three roles of Christ as prophet, priest and king, which he fulfilled during his earthly ministry and continues in the present. Individually and collectively, these offices manifest Christ as the mediator between God and humanity and the fulfillment of Israel's story and hope. Originally articulated by Eusebius, the early church historian, the explanation of these offices was further developed by John *Calvin in his *Institutes.* The *Heidelberg Catechism links the three offices of Christ to Christian vocation and *mission since the Spirit equips Christians to participate in the *kingdom work inaugurated by Jesus.

Torrance, Thomas Forsyth (1913–2007). Scottish Reformed theologian. Born to missionaries in China, Torrance influenced Scottish theology through his work in the Church of Scotland and professorship at New College, Edinburgh. Influenced by his teachers Karl *Barth, John Macmurray, H. R. Mackintosh and A. E. Taylor, he developed his theology around three loci: the relational nature of knowledge, the contingent order of the created world and the definitive action of the triune God in the incarnation. Throughout his career, he maintained an ecumenical outlook by engaging the early church fathers and expositing the Nicene Creed. His major works deal with theological method (*Theological Science*), the Trinity (*Trinitarian Faith*), and the incarnation and *atonement (*The Mediation of Christ*).

total depravity. The first tenet of *TULIP, emphasizing the totality of humanity's broken relationship with God and consequent compromised relationship with the rest of creation. A result of *original sin, total depravity reminds us that every person is born with his or her entire nature corrupted by *sin and at enmity with God. Sin thus affects not merely a person's will but also her or his affections, mind and body: *total* is meant to claim not that fallen humans are as bad as they could be but that there is no aspect of their being that is unaffected by sin. Therefore, just as sin taints every part of our humanity, so *sanctification by God's Spirit ultimately works on every aspect until there is unhindered communion with God in our *glorification.

tradition. *Doctrines and practices transmitted and received by the church as authentic expressions of *faith. While rejecting the Roman Catholic view that the *papacy determines the parameters of tradition, Reformed *orthodoxy normally defends the importance of a core gospel tradition or rule of faith (*regula fidei*) as well as subsidiary traditions articulated in *confessions and embodied in everyday practices. Yet even as it places high value on tradition, it also unapologetically maintains the necessity of continual reform (*semper reformanda*). While recognizing the potential errancy of human traditions and the importance of *sola scriptura*, heirs of the *Reformation demonstrated attentiveness to tradition by, for instance, robustly affirming the *trinitarian theology and *Christology articulated in the first ecumenical creeds. And even when a particular doctrine or practice was deemed unbiblical (e.g., purgatory, indulgences), the Reformers also maintained the vital importance of demonstrating their rejection in patristic sources. In this way, they confirmed the primacy of Scripture and yet maintained the abiding value of the testimony of the *saints.

translation, biblical. The practice of translating the text of the Bible into the vernacular, influenced by the humanist value of returning to original sources (*ad fontes*) and motivated by a passion for *sola scriptura* and the *priesthood of all believers. Even before the *Reformation, John *Wyclif worked tirelessly in translating the Bible from the original languages into his native tongue. Later, *Luther's German Bible translation was a stunning literary achievement, celebrated as a profound contribution to the Reformation and to German culture in general. His work also influenced William *Tyndale, a leading Reformer and the most important English-speaking translator in history. A large portion of the Geneva Bible (1557) and as much as 90 percent of the 1611 King James Version of the New Testament is Tyndale's work, and the same probably would be true of the Old Testament if he had not been executed in 1536 before completing his work. Faithful Bible translation and exegesis became a cornerstone in the *education of Reformed pastors and theologians, many of whom were and continue to be involved in large-scale translation projects.

transubstantiation. The Roman Catholic understanding of the *Lord's Supper, in which the bread and wine are transformed into the body and blood of Jesus Christ during the consecration of the *mass. The belief is that as the priest performs a prayer, the substance or essence of the bread and wine is changed into the actual body and blood of Christ. Nonetheless, there is no change in the accidents, or physical attributes, of the elements. The Reformers rejected the Aristotelian metaphysics assumed by the distinction between substance and accidents, along with the emphasis placed on *sacerdotalism. Instead they offered alternative proposals, represented by *consubstantiation, *real presence and *memorialism.

trinitarian theology. The study of God as one being in three persons—Father, Son and Holy Spirit—as affirmed by the ecumenical creeds. Several Reformed theologians, however, have emphasized distinctive themes within trinitarian theology. A few examples will suffice: some scholars note that John *Calvin reflects the Eastern tradition more than the Western by emphasizing the three persons rather than the one divine essence. John *Owen later articulated a trinitarian spirituality in which believers commune with each divine person distinctly through the Father's love, the Son's grace and the Spirit's consolation. In the trinitarian *ethics of Jonathan *Edwards, the Spirit enables believers to reflect the beauty and love of the Father as revealed in the Son. And most recently, Karl *Barth's focus on triune redemption is intrinsically linked to triune *election and *revelation, centered on the person and work of Christ.

TULIP. An acronym purporting to summarize the major doctrines affirmed by *Calvinists at the Synod of *Dort in opposition to *Arminianism: *total depravity, unconditional *election, limited *atonement, *irresistible grace and *perseverance of the saints. It is important to note, however, that although references can be found to the *five points of Calvinism in the nineteenth century, this precise acronym did not enter circulation until the early twentieth century. In addition, several of these phrases may be understood in ways that misrepresent the *doctrine delineated at Dordrecht. For example, rather than limiting what Christ accomplished by his death on the cross, the Canons of Dort focused on God's particular redemption of the elect through this efficacious event. Furthermore, instead of advocating irresistible grace, which connotes a God who forces people to believe against their will, the canons emphasized God's *effectual calling and *grace that persuasively enliven and incline people to trust in Jesus. Because of these discrepancies, some theologians observe that TULIP leans more toward *hyper-Calvinism instead of providing an accurate description of the historic Reformed tradition. Consequently, many contemporary Reformed theologians have chosen either to employ other acronyms or to use this acronym cautiously and with necessary qualification.

Turretin, Francis (1623–1687). A Swiss Calvinist theologian. Born in Geneva, Turretin received a thorough education in several places, including Geneva, Leiden, Utrecht and Paris. In 1647, he became pastor of an Italian Protestant congregation in Geneva, and several years later became professor of theology at the Geneva Academy. His best-known publication, the four-volume *Institutes of Elenctic Theology* (1679–1685), was an important work in Reformed *scholasticism. Although Turretin's scholasticism was not widely appreciated in the eighteenth century, the Princeton theologians Archibald *Alexander and Charles *Hodge revived his work in the nineteenth century and used it as a standard text for teaching.

two kingdoms. With links to St. Augustine's *City of God* but more firmly rooted in *Lutheranism, the doctrine of two kingdoms holds that God rules the world in two ways or by means of "two kingdoms." God rules civil society or his temporal, "earthly kingdom" by means of the compulsory force of law, and he rules his eternal, "spiritual kingdom" and church by means of *special revelation, the gospel and *grace. Most *neo-Calvinists interpret God's rule differently through the lens of *sphere sovereignty, but other Reformed theologians adopt a perspective more similar to the Lutheran perspective and defend the *spirituality of the church.

Tyndale, William (1494–1536). An English Reformer, a martyr and the single greatest translator of the Bible into the English language. Educated at Oxford and Cambridge, Tyndale's passion was to make the Scriptures available to ordinary people. It is estimated that as much as ninety percent of the 1611 King James or Authorized Version of the New Testament was taken from Tyndale's earlier work and somewhat less from his *translation of the Old Testament, which was never completed because of his execution outside Brussels on false charges of heresy.

U

ubiquity of Christ. A phrase from Martin *Luther's *Christology, according to which God's omnipresence is communicated to Jesus' humanity at his ascension. Luther argues that upon his session, Jesus shares the Father's omnipresence, and he describes Jesus' humanity as a drop of fresh water falling into the salty sea of divinity. This ubiquity provides the basis for *consubstantiation in *Lutheranism's view of the *Lord's Supper. The Reformed tradition rejected this view in order to avoid a confusion of Christ's two natures (*extra calvinisticum*). Interpreting the right hand of God as an actual place, *Calvin sought to preserve the integrity of Jesus' bodily existence in light of his physical return. Along these lines, the Reformed tradition normally seeks to avoid compromising the full humanity of Christ, a truth they fear is lost in a classic Lutheran view of the Lord's Supper.

union with Christ. Also called identification with Christ, a phrase describing the whole scope of *salvation in which believers participate in and receive the benefits of Christ's life, death, resurrection, ascension, session and glorification. John *Calvin emphasized union with Christ as the ground of *justification and *regeneration, but opposed Andreas *Osiander's view that believers participate ontologically in God's essence since the Holy Spirit functions as the bond between believers and Christ. Later Reformed theologians, such as John *Owen, likewise stressed the trinitarian structure of this *doctrine and affirmed *baptism as the sign of covenantal union with Christ.

universal calling. The universal or general call that goes out to every human as an invitation to *repentance and *faith, as distinguished from God's *effectual calling of individuals to *salvation. John *Calvin used the term to describe an external call delivered through the *preaching of God's *Word, but which may be resisted and will not accomplish salvation unless accompanied by God's effectual calling. Sometimes this language is expressed through the phrase "the free offer of the gospel," which goes out indiscriminately to all. It can also refer to the manifestation of God's person and presence to all through *general revelation and *providence.

Ursinus, Zacharias (1534–1584). A Reformed theologian born in Breslau, best known as one of the authors of the *Heidelberg Catechism. Ursinus began his studies at the University of Wittenberg, where he was influenced by Philipp *Melanchthon. In 1561, after a time of study in Zurich with Peter Martyr *Vermigli, he became a professor of theology at Heidelberg University. Together with Caspar Olevianus, in 1562 Ursinus wrote the Heidelberg Catechism, known for its consistent Reformed *doctrine and invitingly warm devotional tone. In addition, Ursinus was responsible for writing all the major confessional documents of the Palatinate (i.e., German Reformed) Church.

Ussher, James. *See* Irish Articles of Religion. *See also* Irish Reformation; Puritanism.

V

Van Til, Cornelius (1895–1987). A Dutch Reformed theologian, philosopher and Presbyterian churchman best known for his *presuppositional approach to *apologetics. Born in Grootegast, Holland, Van Til spent his life and teaching career in the United States. After spending a year at Calvin Theological Seminary, where he studied under Louis *Berkhof, Van Til transferred to Princeton Theological Seminary, where he became friends with Geerhardus *Vos and completed his studies. After teaching for a brief period at Princeton, Van Til, together with J. Gresham *Machen and other scholars concerned with encroaching liberalism, contributed to the founding of Westminster Theological Seminary, where he taught *systematic theology and apologetics for over forty-five years.

Vermigli, Pietro Martire (Peter Martyr) (1499–1562). Florentine humanist and Protestant theologian. Vermigli began in the Augustinian order, studying scholastic philosophy in Padua. After his *ordination in 1525, Vermigli worked with many reform-minded Catholics in Italy. With the Inquisition in 1542, he fled to Strasbourg, where he joined Martin *Bucer and taught Old Testament. In 1548, he went to England at *Cranmer's invitation and was an important influence advocating the *English Reformation, although after Mary Tudor's succession in 1553, he was forced to return to Strasbourg. Vermigli published prolifically during his life, including many biblical commentaries, and after his death a single collection of his *Loci Communes* was compiled, which went through more than a dozen editions.

via antiqua. A medieval theological movement meaning "the old way" in Latin, also called *schola Augustiniana moderna* (the modern Augustinian school). This movement developed during late medieval scholasticism in the fourteenth and fifteenth centuries. Gregory of Rimini and Thomas Bradwardine were the main proponents, articulating their position in direct response to the *via moderna* and stressing that *salvation is totally and completely God's work and not based on any human *merit. In this way, *via antiqua* fundamentally rejected all forms of *Pelagianism, embracing instead a robust *Augustinianism. This movement contributed to the accentuation of *sola gratia* and *justification by faith during the Protestant *Reformation.

via moderna. A medieval theological movement meaning "the modern way" in Latin. This late medieval scholastic movement developed in the fourteenth and fifteenth centuries through the influence of Gabriel Biel and William Ockham. The central theological issue for the *via moderna* had to do with the understanding of *justification. The adherents of this school viewed *soteriology in terms of a covenant between God and humanity in which God accepts those who fulfill the conditions of the covenant by "doing their best." Martin *Luther rejected the movement as a form of *Pelagianism, favoring instead the *via antiqua.

visual art. Although a Reformed *theological aesthetic originally limited appreciation of visual art in the context of *worship, the *Reformation also had a positive impact on visual art. For example, the Reformers' emphasis on the dignity of individuals as bearers of the *imago dei corresponds with the concurrent rise of portraiture. Furthermore, viewing creation as the theater of God's glory, as John *Calvin did, inspired both the flowering of Dutch landscape painting and the selection of more mundane subject matter. Additionally, belief in humanity's *total depravity along with God's sovereign *grace in *salvation is evident in the hopeful realism of a painter like Rembrandt van Rijn.

vocational calling. Growing out of the *Reformation, this concept emphasized the call of God into a particular kind of work or situation in life as an opportunity to express Christian obedience to the glory of God. Prior to the Reformation, although theologians affirmed God's call to his people for *salvation, it was common to consider only the *clergy as those divinely called and gifted to a particular vocation. Reformers like *Luther and *Calvin, however, opposed this view and argued that all believers are called to various vocations, whether ecclesiastical or secular, and that these callings are equally dignified and capable of bringing glory to God.

Vos, Geerhardus (1862–1947). A Dutch theologian who taught in America, best known for his influence on hermeneutics and *biblical theology. Vos was born in the Netherlands, but his family came to America when Vos was nineteen, and his father became pastor of a Christian Reformed Church in Grand Rapids, Michigan. Vos attended the Theologische School (later Calvin Theological Seminary), Princeton Seminary and then did postgraduate work in Germany. He taught at the Theologische School until 1893, when he became professor of biblical theology at Princeton Seminary. While at Princeton, Vos developed his biblical theology, emphasizing how theology develops organically and progressively within the eschatological story of redemption presented in Scripture.

W

Waldensians. A movement arising out of the Roman Catholic Church in twelfth-century Italy. Its founder was a man named Valdes (anglicized as Peter Waldo), who, after *conversion, gave all his wealth to the poor and began living on alms and *preaching. In 1179 the pope approved his activity on condition that he and his followers would not preach without permission from *clergy. When they broke this rule several years later, they were excommunicated and treated as heretics, despite the fact that they professed orthodox belief. Scattered throughout central Europe, many Waldensians established links with the Protestant *Reformation, and to a large extent the movement was absorbed into other Protestant groups. A small Waldensian strand did remain, however, and several churches bearing this name still exist today.

Warfield, Benjamin B. (1851–1921). *Presbyterian professor of theology at Princeton Seminary and advocate of what is now known as *Princeton theology. Warfield served as editor of the *Princeton Review* and was appointed professor of didactic and polemical theology, succeeding A. A. Hodge. Warfield was a great apologist and focused much of his energy on defending the doctrine of biblical inerrancy. He was a prolific writer, and his works include influential pieces such as *Introduction to the Textual Criticism of the New Testament* and "Inspiration," an article in the *Princeton Review* coauthored with A. A. Hodge.

Watts, Isaac (1674–1748). English pastor, author and hymn writer, often called the father of English hymnody. Raised within the *Puritan tradition, Watts became minister of an independent church in London. As a young pastor, he became ill and remained in poor health for the rest of his life. Nevertheless, he was a prolific writer on a variety of philosophical and theological topics, and best remembered for his composition of hundreds of hymns, often using extrabiblical poetry. Watts's work wielded widespread influence on *worship within the Reformed tradition and *evangelicalism, especially in the practice of singing hymns together with psalms in corporate worship.

Westminster Assembly (1643–1649). The Westminster Assembly of Divines was the largest parliamentary committee during the English Civil War. It was convened by the Parliament and without the king's permission for the purpose of reforming the Church of England. The assembly, which included members of the House of Lords and House of Commons as well as clergymen from across Britain, first met on July 1, 1643, in Westminster Abbey. *Presbyterian, Independent and Erastian clergy debated over issues of *doctrine, church *polity, *liturgy and *worship, and a possible union of the Churches of England and Scotland. The assembly produced the *Westminster Standards, which were adopted by the General Assembly of the Scottish Church and to varying degrees by the English and Scottish Houses of Parliament. After these standards were published, the assembly continued to serve as a committee to examine candidates for *ordination and deal with other ecclesiological issues until its dissolution in 1649.

Westminster Standards. The confessional documents drawn up by the *Westminster Assembly (1643–1649). The standards include the Westminster Confession of Faith (1646), Larger and Shorter Catechisms (1647), Directory for the Public Worship of God (1644), and Form of Presbyterian Church Government (1645). They continue in use as constitutional documents in several contemporary Reformed denominations around the world.

Whitefield, George (1714–1770). An English preacher who influenced the *Great Awakening in colonial America. After his conversion at Oxford, Whitefield became friends with John and Charles Wesley, though he would eventually disagree with them theologically. In 1738, Whitefield was ordained and quickly gained notoriety for his animated *preaching, sometimes gathering crowds as large as twenty thousand. His trip to America in 1740 advanced the Great Awakening. Although not a trained theologian, Whitefield was committed to a basic form of *Calvinism while sharing with the *Arminian Wesleys an emphasis on Spirit-enabled *regeneration and *justification by faith through Christ. He died on a preaching tour in New England in 1770.

Witherspoon, John (1723–1794). A Scottish *Presbyterian most remembered for his political leadership during the founding of the United States. As a young pastor in Scotland, he was particularly committed to counteracting the church's tendency to be dominated by rich landowners. In 1768 he emigrated to the colonies, where he became the sixth president of the College of New Jersey (Princeton). He taught many important American statesmen, including James Madison, but Witherspoon was less influential as an intellectual than as a public figure. He supported civic republicanism, signed the Declaration of Independence and voted to ratify the American Constitution. As a churchman, he was active in establishing the Presbyterian Church in the United States of America and in its adoption of the *Westminster Standards.

Woosley, Louisa Mariah Layman (1862–1952). The first woman to be ordained (1889) and officially recognized as such by a Reformed denomination. Woosley pursued this call after studying the role of women in the Bible, and the result of this study was published to defend her ministry in the article "Shall Woman Preach?" After her *ordination and after overcoming initial opposition, she served as a minister of the Cumberland Presbyterian Church for forty-five years. Her tireless work included serving as a pastor of several churches in her native Kentucky, as an evangelist across several American states and as a commissioner at the General Assembly of the CPC.

Word of God. The various meanings of this theological concept reflect its diverse use in Scripture. It can refer to the *canon of Scripture, *revelation, *preaching or the second person of the Trinity. John *Calvin's emphasis on the *logos* *Christology of John's Gospel has been foundational for Reformed *orthodoxy in the *doctrines of the *providence of God, *election and *extra calvinisticum*. For Herman *Bavinck and Karl *Barth, the identification of the Word with *special revelation has a prominent place at the beginning of *systematic theology, which challenges attempts to gain *knowledge of God by any other means.

work. A Reformed perspective affirms work as a gift from God rooted in creation while recognizing the enduring effects of the fall. Work brings glory to God and advances the common good, but is also susceptible to corruption. Believers must therefore rely on the Spirit to fulfill their *vocational callings. *Neo-Calvinists such as Abraham *Kuyper and Herman *Dooyeweerd expanded on this notion by identifying various spheres of life governed by creational norms, which provide guidelines for faithful work. The work ethic arising out of *Protestantism, as Max Weber famously argued, may have influenced the rise of capitalism, but the Reformed tradition has typically urged caution in identifying biblical Christianity with one economic model.

World Alliance of Reformed Churches (WARC). In 1970, the World Presbyterian Alliance (1875) and the International Congregational Council (1891) united to form the WARC. It was based in Geneva, Switzerland, and had a strong relationship with the World Council of Churches. Many of the 214 churches in 107 countries were also members of the *Reformed Ecumenical Council (REC), and the WARC represented a wide spectrum of Reformed churches whose stances regarding *doctrine, *social action and *ecumenism varied greatly. Outwardly focused, it facilitated numerous ecumenical forums with other major Christian traditions and took a strong stance against apartheid in South Africa. In 2010, it merged with the REC to become the *World Communion of Reformed Churches (WCRC).

World Communion of Reformed Churches (WCRC). In June 2010, the *World Alliance of Reformed Churches (WARC) and the *Reformed Ecumenical Council (REC) merged to create the largest international fellowship of Reformed, *Presbyterian, *Congregational, *Waldensian, United and Uniting churches. The WCRC represents eighty million Christians in 108 countries and maintains ecumenical links with the World Council of Churches and other international Christian communions. While continuing as a forum for internal discussions of Reformed identity, the WCRC focuses on the contributions of the Reformed tradition to the growth of the catholic church, interfaith discussions and *social action. Its international office is the former WARC office in Geneva, Switzerland, and its American office is the former REC office in Grand Rapids, Michigan.

worldview. A framework of concepts and values that enable understanding and engagement of the world. The term comes from the German *Weltanschauung*, originally coined by Immanuel Kant in his *Critique of Judgment* (1790). It began to appear in *Reformed theology at the end of the nineteenth century through the works of James *Orr, Herman *Dooyeweerd and Abraham *Kuyper, and later shaped the landscape of *evangelicalism through the influence of Francis *Schaeffer and Carl *Henry. As a concept encouraging Christian reflection on every area of life, worldview thinking has wielded enormous influence on *education and perspectives on *Christ and culture within the Reformed tradition and beyond.

worship. As the act of responding to God in gratitude and adoration, worship normally refers to liturgical expressions of praise, whether public or private, as well as the overall pattern of Christian *piety. The Reformers were adamant that public and private worship maintain biblical integrity and avoid *idolatry, which motivated them to construct simple and intelligible *liturgy oriented toward edification. Although perspectives varied with respect to the role of *music in worship, *preaching and the *sacraments have always played a central role in Reformed worship, given the overall emphasis in *Reformed theology on *Word and Spirit. Even today, great diversity of worship forms and styles exists within the global Reformed tradition.

Wyclif, John (c. 1330–1384). English theologian and Oxford professor, often referred to as the morning star of the *Reformation. Wyclif's belief in the absolute authority of Scripture led him to oversee the *translation of the Bible into the English vernacular of the time. His own study of Scripture led him to oppose *transubstantiation, monasticism, the mediatory power of the priest and other Catholic *doctrines, resulting in his dismissal from Oxford. However, his influence had already spread from Oxford to continental Europe, most notably the Bohemian theologian Jan *Hus. Wyclif's English followers, called Lollards, gained strength and were even represented in Parliament for a time before undergoing extreme persecution in the fifteenth century.

X, Y, Z

Zell, Katherina Schütz (c. 1497–1562). Protestant Reformer and author in Strasbourg remembered for her acts of charity to the poor and persecuted. Well educated for women of the time, Zell wrote in the German vernacular; her inability to write in Latin made her works accessible to the laity. Married to the Reformer Matthew Zell, she worked together with him in showing hospitality and maintaining friendship even with those they disagreed with theologically. Her writings include a defense of the rights of Protestant *clergy to marry, a hymnal, and works of devotional and practical value addressing pressing issues within the church.

Zwingli, Ulrich (Huldrych) (1484–1531). One of the primary fathers of the Protestant *Reformation, along with *Luther and *Calvin. Born in German-speaking Switzerland, Zwingli was educated at Basel and Vienna, where he was greatly influenced by the *humanism of the northern Renaissance and the teaching of Desiderius *Erasmus, with whom he later corresponded. Even after he completed his formal degree, Zwingli continued to further his humanist and theological studies, attending lectures by Thomas Wyttenbach, whose teaching helped lay the foundation for Zwingli's beliefs in the authority of Scripture and *justification by faith. He was ordained as a priest in the Roman Catholic Church in 1506 and called to the parish of Glarus, which served as a prominent center for the Swiss government to recruit Swiss soldiers for hire to assist the war campaigns of other political entities. Except for those campaigns that were done on behalf of the pope, Zwingli opposed this system of mercenary service. At various times between 1512 and 1516, he served as chaplain for the papal mercenary service, which gave him the opportunity to travel in Italy, where he began to see discrepancies between contemporary Catholic practices and ancient ones he found in earlier Italian masses. By the end of his chaplaincy, he regarded papal mercenary service as inappropriate, but his service as a chaplain placed him in good standing with the papacy for years to come. He continued his private studies as a parish priest, even teaching himself Greek, and his last year of service at Glarus, 1516, is the year Zwingli himself noted that he came to a Reformed understanding of Scripture. In 1516 he officially transferred to Einsiedeln, a popular pilgrimage site with a shrine to Mary, where many pilgrims had an opportunity to hear his *preaching. Zwingli was appointed to serve as priest at Grossmünster in Zurich in 1519, despite objections by some due to his known history of unchastity while at Einsiedeln, which he confessed to and found the strength to combat through his increasingly Reformed beliefs. At Grossmünster, he began systematically preaching through the New Testament, during which time his support of Luther and the increasingly popular *doctrines of the Reformation became more evident. He began decrying the Catholic practices and doctrines of monasticism, *purgatory, pilgrimages, veneration of Mary and *indulgences.

Still remembered today for the emphasis he placed on Scripture's ultimate authority, Zwingli assisted with the publication of the Züricher Bible (1529), one of the earliest *translations into the German vernacular. As his leadership developed, Zwingli came into conflict at certain points with Martin *Luther, particularly with respect to their different understandings of the presence of Christ in the *Lord's Supper. This was the central issue when they met at the *Marburg Colloquy, where Zwingli advocated *memorialism as opposed to Luther's *consubstantiation. Zwingli also strongly supported secular state authority, much to the chagrin of some *Anabaptists who were initially inspired by him. He ensured that the local government approved all changes within the church, and as the *Swiss Reformation progressed, some cantons adopted Zwingli's suggestions and enforced Protestantism, forbidding the *mass and other practices deemed unbiblical, which led to conflict and war with the Catholic-supporting cantons. It was at the Battle of Kappel, while leading Zurich's troops against Catholic armies, that Zwingli was killed in October 1531. Heinrich *Bullinger served as his successor in leading the church in Zurich, as well as filling his position at Grossmünster.

Zwinglianism. A branch of the Reformed tradition tracing its roots back to Ulrich *Zwingli and Heinrich *Bullinger. Bullinger, as the successor of Zwingli and primary promoter of his teachings despite minor disagreements, was instrumental in the development and spread of Zwinglianism beyond the borders of Switzerland, where it first developed. While Zwinglianism had a wide impact, it was most influential in Switzerland, southwest Germany, Holland, England and Scotland. It is distinct from *Lutheranism and *Calvinism primarily as a result of its views on the *Lord's Supper, the Christian community and *predestination. Zwingli's disagreements with *Luther regarding the Lord's Supper culminated in the *Marburg Colloquy of 1529, and remained unresolved. The Calvinists and Zwinglians, however, came to an agreement on the issue in the Consensus Tigurinus of 1549. Both Lutherans and Calvinists disagreed with a Zwinglian understanding of how the Christian community should be ruled by Christian civil *government. Bullinger's *covenant theology viewed the Old Testament pattern of kings ruling over and leading God's people as a model for contemporary Christian civil government, and he rejected the need for separate ecclesiastical courts. The disagreements over predestination stemmed from rejection among Zwinglians of Calvin's double decree and an emphasis on *universal calling. Despite these differences, however, Bullinger and other Zwinglians often maintained close ties with Calvinists, and influences of Zwinglianism can still be seen in Calvinism. Zwinglianism was a prominent force in the Reformed tradition from the time of Zwingli until the late sixteenth century, after which time mainstream Zwinglianism was mostly eclipsed by Calvinism.

Bibliography

Below is a bibliography to help the reader become better acquainted with the Reformed tradition. We begin with general reference works that provide further background and introductory works that give a sense of the overall landscape of the Reformed heritage. Such volumes have been extremely helpful in our own composition of this book.

We have also provided a sampling of Reformed theology from the Reformation to the present, organizing this section according to time periods. We have certainly not tried to be comprehensive, but we have attempted to present the breadth of the tradition and to offer a taste for some of the most significant works across the spectrum. Inevitably, depending on one's location within this tradition, one may wish we had included some volumes or left others out. While recognizing such opinions, our goal here is to provide the interested reader with a genuine sampling of key and varied Reformed expressions from the last five centuries and to encourage the exploration of original sources. We hope to that end that this list proves helpful.

Select Reference Works

Benedetto, Robert, and Donald McKim. *Historical Dictionary of the Reformed Churches*. 2nd ed. Lanham, MD: Scarecrow, 2010.

Christian Classics Ethereal Library: www.ccel.org.

Elwell, Walter A. *Evangelical Dictionary of Theology*. Grand Rapids: Baker Books, 1984.

Fahlbusch, Erwin, et al., eds. *The Encyclopedia of Christianity*. Translated by Geoffrey W. Bromiley. 5 vols. Grand Rapids: Eerdmans, 1999–2008.

Grenz, Stanley, David Guretski and Cherith Fee Nordling. *Pocket Dictionary of Theological Terms*. Downers Grove, IL: InterVarsity Press, 1999.

Hart, Daryl G., and Mark A. Noll. *Dictionary of the Presbyterian and Reformed Tradition in America*. Phillipsburg, NJ: P&R, 2005.

Hart, Trevor A., ed. *The Dictionary of Historical Theology*. Grand Rapids: Eerdmans, 2000.

Hillerbrand, Hans J. *The Encyclopedia of Protestantism*. 4 vols. New York: Routledge, 2004.

———. *The Oxford Encyclopedia of the Reformation*. 4 vols. New York: Oxford University Press, 1996.

McKim, Donald. *The Westminster Handbook to Reformed Theology*. Louisville, KY: Westminster John Knox, 2001.

McKim, Donald, and David F. Wright, eds. *Encyclopedia of the Reformed Faith*. Edinburgh: Saint Andrew Press, 1992.

Muller, Richard A. *Dictionary of Latin and Greek Theological Terms: Drawn Principally from Protestant Scholastic Theology*. Grand Rapids: Baker Books, 1985.

Picken, Stuart D. B. *Historical Dictionary of Calvinism*. Lanham, MD: Scarecrow, 2012.

Helpful Introductory Literature

Allen, Michael R. *Reformed Theology*. London: T & T Clark, 2010.

Alston, Wallace M., Jr., and Michael Welker, eds. *Reformed Theology: Identity and Ecumenicity*. Grand Rapids: Eerdmans, 2003.

Benedict, Philip. *Christ's Churches Purely Reformed: A Social History of Calvinism*. New Haven, CT: Yale University Press, 2002.

Carter, Anthony J. *On Being Black and Reformed: A New Perspective on the African-American Christian Experience*. Phillipsburg, NJ: P&R, 2003.

DeGruchy, John. *Liberating Reformed Theology: A South African Contribution to an Ecumenical Debate*. Grand Rapids: Eerdmans, 1991.

Gerrish, B. A., ed. *Reformed Theology for the Third Christian Millennium: The Sprunt Lectures 2001*. Louisville, KY: Westminster John Knox, 2003.

Guthrie, Shirley C., Jr. *Always Being Reformed: Faith for a Fragmented World*. Louisville, KY: Westminster John Knox, 2008.

Hansen, Collin. *Young, Restless, Reformed: A Journalist's Journey with the New Calvinists*. Wheaton, IL: Crossway, 2008.

Hyde, Daniel. *Welcome to a Reformed Church: A Guide for Pilgrims*. Sanford, FL: Reformation Trust, 2010.

Johnson, William Stacy, and John H. Leith, eds. *Reformed Reader: A Sourcebook in Christian Theology*. Vol. 1, *Classical Beginnings, 1519–1799*. Louisville, KY: Westminster John Knox, 1993.

Lane, Belden C. *Ravished by Beauty: The Surprising Legacy of Reformed Spirituality*. New York: Oxford University Press, 2011.

Lucas, Sean Michael. *On Being Presbyterian: Our Beliefs, Practices, and Stories*. Phillipsburg, NJ: P&R, 2006.

McGrath, Alister E. *Reformation Thought: An Introduction* [1988]. 4th ed. Malden, MA: Wiley-Blackwell, 2012.

McKim, Donald K. *Introducing the Reformed Faith: Biblical Revelation, Christian Tradition, Contemporary Significance*. Louisville, KY: Westminster John Knox, 2001.

Mouw, Richard J. *Calvinism in the Las Vegas Airport: Making Connections in Today's World*. Grand Rapids: Zondervan, 2004.

Muller, Richard A. *Post-Reformation Reformed Dogmatics: The Rise and Development of Reformed Orthodoxy, Ca. 1520 to Ca. 1725.* 2nd ed. 4 vols. Grand Rapids: Baker Academic, 2003.

Rohls, Jan. *Reformed Confessions: Theology from Zurich to Barmen.* Columbia Series in Reformed Theology. Louisville, KY: Westminster John Knox, 1998.

Smith, James K. A. *Letters to a Young Calvinist: An Invitation to the Reformed Tradition.* Grand Rapids: Brazos, 2010.

Stewart, Kenneth J. *Ten Myths About Calvinism: Recovering the Breadth of the Reformed Tradition.* Downers Grove, IL: IVP Academic, 2011.

Stroup, George, ed. *Reformed Reader: A Sourcebook in Christian Theology.* Vol. 2, *Contemporary Trajectories 1799–Present.* Louisville, KY: Westminster John Knox, 1993.

Torrance, Thomas F., ed. *The School of Faith: The Catechisms of the Reformed Church.* London: James Clarke & Co., 1959.

Wells, David F., ed. *Reformed Theology in America: A History of Its Modern Development.* Grand Rapids: Eerdmans, 1985.

Willis-Watkins, David, and Michael Welker, eds. *Toward the Future of Reformed Theology: Tasks, Topics, Traditions.* Grand Rapids: Eerdmans, 1998.

Wolters, Al. *Creation Regained: Biblical Basis for a Reformational Worldview* [1985]. 2nd ed. Grand Rapids: Eerdmans, 2005.

A Sampling of Classic Works from the Reformed Tradition

Sixteenth Century

Beza, Theodore. *Confession of the Christian Faith* [1558, French]. Translated by James Clark. East Essex: Focus Christian Ministries Trust, 1992.

Bucer, Martin. *The Kingdom of Christ* [1558, Latin]. In *Melancthon and Bucer*, edited by Wilhelm Pauck. Library of Christian Classics 24. Louisville, KY: Westminster John Knox, 1969.

Bullinger, Heinrich. *The Decades of Henry Bullinger* [1552, French]. Edited by Thomas Harding, Parker Society. Cambridge: Cambridge University Press, 1849–1852. Reprint, 4 books in 2, Grand Rapids: Reformation Heritage Books, 2004.

Calvin, John. *Institutes of the Christian Religion* [1536–1559/60, Latin]. 2 vols. Library of Christian Classics. Philadelphia: Westminster, 1960.

Perkins, William. *A Golden Chaine* [1590, Latin]. In *The Work of William Perkins*, edited by Ian Breward. Courtenay Library of Reformation Classics 3. Abingdon: Sutton Courtenay, 1970.

Ursinus, Zacharias. *Commentary on the Heidelberg Catechism* [1589, German]. Phillipsburg, NJ: P&R, 1992.

Vermigli, Pietro Martire. *Predestination and Justification: Two Theological Loci* [1558, Latin]. Translated by Frank A. James. Sixteenth Century Essays & Studies 68. Kirksville, MO: Truman State University Press, 2003.

Zwingli, Ulrich. *In Search of True Religion* [1525, German]. In *Huldrych Zwingli: Writings.* 2 vols. Pittsburgh Theological Monographs. Allison Park, PA: Pickwick, 1984.

Seventeenth and Eighteenth Centuries

Ames, William. *The Marrow of Theology* [1623]. Edited by John Dykstra Eusden. Grand Rapids: Baker Books, 1997.

Baxter, Richard. *The Saints' Everlasting Rest* [1654]. Edited by John Thomas Wilkinson. Foreword by J. I. Packer. Vancouver: Regent College Publishing, 2004.

Bunyan, John. *Pilgrim's Progress* [1678]. Edited by Roger Pooley. New York: Penguin Classics, 2009.

Edwards, Jonathan. *Freedom of the Will* [1754]. Edited by Paul Ramsey. Vol. 1 of *The Works of Jonathan Edwards*. New Haven, CT: Yale University Press, 1957.

———. *Original Sin* [1758]. Edited by Clyde A. Holbrook. Vol. 3 of *The Works of Jonathan Edwards*. New Haven, CT: Yale University Press, 1970.

Owen, John. *Communion with the Triune God* [1657]. Edited by Kelly M. Kapic and Justin Taylor. Wheaton, IL: Crossway, 2007.

———. *Overcoming Sin and Temptation* [1656, 1658, 1667]. Edited by Kelly M. Kapic and Justin Taylor. Wheaton, IL: Crossway, 2006.

Rutherford, Samuel. *Letters of Samuel Rutherford* [1664]. Edinburgh: Banner of Truth Trust, 1973.

Turretin, Francis. *Institutes of Elenctic Theology* [1679–1685, Latin]. Translated by George Musgrave Giger. Edited by James T. Dennison. 3 vols. Phillipsburg, NJ: P&R, 1992.

Voetius, Gisbertus. "Concerning Practical Theology" [1648–1659, Latin]. In *Reformed Dogmatics: J. Wollebius, G. Voetius and F. Turretin*, edited and translated by John W. Beardslee. Library of Protestant Thought. New York: Oxford University Press, 1965.

Witsius, Hermann. *The Economy of the Covenants Between God and Man* [1677, Latin]. Phillipsburg, NJ: P&R, 1990.

Wollebius, Johannes. "Compendium of Christian Theology" [1626, Latin]. In *Reformed Dogmatics: J. Wollebius, G. Voetius and F. Turretin*, edited and translated by John W. Beardslee. Library of Protestant Thought. New York: Oxford University Press, 1965.

Nineteenth to Mid-twentieth Centuries

Bavinck, Herman. *Reformed Dogmatics* [1895–1899, Dutch]. Translated by John Vriend. Edited by John Bolt. 4 vols. Grand Rapids: Baker Academic, 2003–2008.

Berkhof, Louis. *Systematic Theology* [1932]. Grand Rapids: Eerdmans, 1994.

Dabney, Robert Louis. *Systematic Theology* [1871]. Edinburgh: Banner of Truth Trust, 1985.

Forsyth, P. T. *The Cruciality of the Cross* [1909]. London: Independent Press, 1948.

Heppe, Heinrich. *Reformed Dogmatics* [1861, German]. Translated by G. T. Thomson. Edited by Ernst Bizer. Grand Rapids: Baker Books, 1978.

Hodge, Charles. *Systematic Theology* [1871–1873]. 3 vols. Grand Rapids: Eerdmans, 1952.

Kuyper, Abraham. *Lectures on Calvinism*. Grand Rapids: Eerdmans, 1931.

Machen, J. Gresham. *Christianity and Liberalism*. Grand Rapids: Eerdmans, 1923.

Schleiermacher, Friedrich. *The Christian Faith* [1821–1822; 2nd ed. 1830–1831, German]. Edited by H. R. Mackintosh and J. S. Stewart. London: T & T Clark, 1999.

Shedd, William G. T. *Dogmatic Theology* [1884–1894]. Edited by Alan W. Gomes. Phillipsburg, NJ: P&R, 2003.

Spurgeon, Charles H. *A Defense of Calvinism* [1898]. Edinburgh: Banner of Truth Trust, 2008.

Warfield, Benjamin B. *Biblical Doctrines*. Vol. 2 of *The Works of Benjamin B. Warfield*. New York: Oxford University Press, 1932.

———. *Calvin and Calvinism*. Vol. 5 of *The Works of Benjamin B. Warfield*. New York: Oxford University Press, 1932.

Weber, Otto. *Foundations of Dogmatics* [1895–1901]. 2 vols. Grand Rapids: Eerdmans, 1981–1983.

Mid-twentieth Century to Present

Barth, Karl. *Church Dogmatics* [1932–1967, German]. Translated by G. W. Bromiley. Edited by G. W. Bromiley and T. F. Torrance. 4 vols. Edinburgh: T & T Clark, 1957–1969.

Berkhof, Hendrikus. *Christian Faith: An Introduction to the Study of the Faith* [1973, Dutch]. Translated by Sierd Woudstra. Grand Rapids: Eerdmans, 1979.

Berkouwer, Gerrit Cornelius. *Studies in Dogmatics* [1949–1972, Dutch]. 14 vols. Grand Rapids: Eerdmans, 1952–1976.

Bloesch, Donald G. *Christian Foundations*. 7 vols. Downers Grove, IL: InterVarsity Press, 1992–2004.

Brunner, Emil. *Dogmatics* [1946–1960, German]. 3 vols. Philadelphia: Westminster Press, 1950–1962.

Frame, John. *The Doctrine of the Knowledge of God*. Theology of Lordship 1. Phillipsburg, NJ: P&R, 1987.

Gunton, Colin E. *The Promise of Trinitarian Theology* [1991]. 2nd ed. London: T & T Clark, 2003.

Henry, Carl F. H. *God, Revelation, and Authority* [1976–1983]. 6 vols. Wheaton, IL: Crossway, 1999.

Hoekema, Anthony. *Saved by Grace*. Grand Rapids: Eerdmans, 1994.

Horton, Michael Scott. *The Christian Faith: A Systematic Theology for Pilgrims on the Way*. Grand Rapids: Zondervan, 2011.

Migliore, Daniel. *Faith Seeking Understanding: An Introduction to Christian Theology* [1991]. 2nd ed. Grand Rapids: Eerdmans, 2004.

Moltmann, Jürgen. *Theology of Hope: On the Ground and the Implications of a Christian Eschatology* [1965, German]. Minneapolis: Augsburg Fortress Press, 1993.

Murray, John. *Redemption, Accomplished and Applied* [1955]. Grand Rapids: Eerdmans, 1992.

Niebuhr, H. Richard. *Christ and Culture*. New York: Harper & Row, 1951.

Niebuhr, Reinhold. *The Nature and Destiny of Man: A Christian Interpretation*. New York: Scribner's Sons, 1949.

Packer, J. I. *Knowing God*. Downers Grove, IL: InterVarsity Press, 1973.

Piper, John. *Desiring God: Meditations of a Christian Hedonist*. Portland, OR: Multnomah Press, 1986.

Schaffer, Francis. *How Should We Then Live? The Rise and Decline of Western Thought and Culture* [1976]. 2nd ed. In *The Complete Works of Francis A. Schaeffer*. Wheaton, IL: Crossway, 1985.

Sproul, R. C. *The Holiness of God* [1985]. 2nd ed. Carol Stream, IL: Tyndale, 2000.

Torrance, James B. *Worship, Community and the Triune God of Grace*. Downers Grove, IL: IVP Academic, 1997.

Torrance, Thomas F. *Atonement: The Person and Work of Christ*. Edited by Robert T. Walker. Downers Grove, IL: IVP Academic, 2009.

———. *Incarnation: The Person and Life of Christ*. Edited by Robert T. Walker. Downers Grove, IL: IVP Academic, 2008.

Vanhoozer, Kevin J. *The Drama of Doctrine: A Canonical-Linguistic Approach to Theology*. Louisville, KY: Westminster John Knox, 2005.

Webster, John. *Holiness*. Grand Rapids: Eerdmans, 2003.

Wolterstorff, Nicholas. *Until Justice and Peace Embrace*. Grand Rapids: Eerdmans, 1983.